"According to psychologist and spiritual director Benner, surrendering to God's will is choosing God over self in all areas of life."
Publishers Weekly, December 13, 2004 (starred review)

"David G. Benner has done it again! *Desiring God's Will* is the perfect capstone for one of the finest trilogies of Christian spiritual formation that has ever been written. I recommend it for any serious seeker who desires for his or her heart to resonate in perfect pitch with the heart of God."
Gary W. Moon, director, Martin Family Institute and Dallas Willard Center for Spiritual Formation at Westmont College, and author of *Apprenticeship with Jesus*

"Can it really be that the things I most deeply want point me toward God? Can it be that these same things tell me something about what God deeply wants for me? With hope and clarity, David Benner demonstrates that the answers to these questions are a resounding yes. Psychologically sound and spiritually compelling, this book moves us beyond our fear and suspicion that somehow God's desires for us and ours for ourselves are mutually exclusive, to a path for discerning God's will that is deeply satisfying because it is congruent with our authentic self in God."
Ruth Haley Barton, cofounder, The Transforming Center, spiritual director, and author of *Life Together in Christ*

"David Benner releases us from the burden of having to figure out God's will, which too often becomes an obsession to us. Instead, he invites us to embrace the will of God as we know it for today. Along the way he provides enormously helpful categories: we should be willing but not willful; we should explore our true desires, not dismiss all desire as bad; we should realize that God's will has less to do with a particular decision and more to do with the most important decision we will ever make—to pursue God. I found this short book helpful and insightful. It was obvious that Benner did not write this book on a whim. The material has been simmering in his soul for some time."
Gerald L. Sittser, professor of theology, Whitworth University, and author of *Water from a Deep Well*

"*Desiring God's Will* is a fresh alternative to today's common spiritual writing. David Benner has written a penetrating book, faithful to ancient truth, that goes beyond the facile 'how to' and seeks to confront the heart of our rebellion, independence and pride. This is a welcome gift to those who want to move past easy answers as they surrender to a truly authentic faith and walk with God."
Gary Thomas, author of *Sacred Pathways* and *Sacred Marriage*

"Benner has provided a masterful understanding of God's will that rightly places the emphasis upon a loving, responsive relationship with God rather than the correct performance of a structure of 'duties.' This is one of very few books on Christian spirituality that I couldn't wait to get back to when I had to break off reluctantly for other duties."

M. Robert Mulholland, author of *Invitation to a Journey*

"This is really a wonderful book, a powerful book, a life-giving book—Benner speaks so honestly, openly and directly to our lust for the self-determination and control that keeps us from knowing the joy and freedom of a God-centered life, a life of willingness in response to God's constant personal love. Reading this book I came to know more fully than ever before how much God desires me."

M. Basil Pennington, OCSO, author of *Lectio Divina* and *Centering Prayer*

"In *Desiring God's Will*, the third in his trilogy, David Benner writes in a deeply personal way of the corrective activist Christians need, not so much to seek guidance as to deeply desire God's will. No more important message could be given us in our narcissistic culture. Poignantly written, this is a life-changing book."

James M. Houston, emeritus professor, Regent College, Vancouver

"David Benner never disappoints. He is intelligent without being academic, psychologically astute without being trendy, spiritually profound without being pious. He clearly knows the landscape from which he dares to speak."

Richard Rohr, OFM, Center for Action and Contemplation, Albuquerque, New Mexico

"This is for people who want God. Even more, it is for people who want to want God. It is about not the taming of the will but its transformation."

John Ortberg, author, senior pastor, Menlo Park Presbyterian Church

The Spiritual Journey

*W*hen applied to the spiritual life, the metaphor of a journey is both helpful and somewhat misleading. Helpfully it reflects the fact that the essence of spirituality is a process—specifically, a process of transformation. Unhelpfully it obscures the fact that we are already what we seek and where we long to arrive—specifically, in God. Once we realize this, the nature of the journey reveals itself to be more one of awakening than accomplishment, more one of spiritual awareness than spiritual achievement.

There are, however, two very good reasons to describe the spiritual life in terms of a journey. First, it fits well with our experience. We are aware that the self that begins the spiritual journey is not the same as the one that ends it. The changes in identity and consciousness—how we understand what it means to be me and our inner experience of passing through life—are both sufficiently profound as to be best described as transformational. The same is true for the changes in our capacity for love and the functioning of our will and desires.

The second reason is that the spiritual journey involves following a path. Much more than adopting a set of beliefs, a path is a practice or set of practices that will characterize our whole life. Following this path is the way we participate in our transformation. It is the way we journey into God and, as we do, discover that all along we have already been in God. It is the way our identity, consciousness and life become grounded in our self-in-God and God's self-in-us.

Christian spirituality is taking on the mind and heart of Christ as we recognize Christ as the deepest truth of our being. It is actualizing the Christ who is in us. It is becoming fully and deeply human. It is experiencing and responding to the world through the mind and heart of God as we align ourselves with God's transformational agenda of making all things new in Christ. It is participating in the very life of God.

This trilogy describes the foundational Christian practice of surrender, how this practice emerges as a response to Perfect Love, and the changes this produces in our identity, will and deepest desires. Each of the three books focuses on one of these strands while interweaving it with the others. Together they serve as a manual for walking the spiritual path as God's heart and mind slowly but truly become our own. The Spiritual Journey trilogy includes:

Surrender to Love: Discovering the Heart of Christian Spirituality
The Gift of Being Yourself: The Sacred Call to Self-Discovery
Desiring God's Will: Aligning Our Hearts with the Heart of God

DESIRING GOD'S WILL

Aligning Our Hearts with the Heart of God

Expanded Edition

DAVID G. BENNER

Foreword by THOMAS H. GREEN, SJ

IVP Books

An imprint of InterVarsity Press
Downers Grove, Illinois

InterVarsity Press
P.O. Box 1400, Downers Grove, IL 60515-1426
ivpress.com
email@ivpress.com

Expanded Edition ©2015 by David G. Benner
First Edition ©2005 by David G. Benner

InterVarsity Press® is the book-publishing division of InterVarsity Christian Fellowship/USA®, a movement of students and faculty active on campus at hundreds of universities, colleges and schools of nursing in the United States of America, and a member movement of the International Fellowship of Evangelical Students. For information about local and regional activities, visit intervarsity.org.

Scripture is taken from the Jerusalem Bible, copyright © 1966 by Darton, Longman & Todd, Ltd. and Doubleday, a division of Bantam Doubleday Dell Publishing Group, Inc. Reprinted by permission.

While any stories in this book are true, some names and identifying information may have been changed to protect the privacy of individuals.

Cover design: Cindy Kiple
Interior design: Beth McGill
Images: The Woodpecker Tapestry, William Morris / Private Collection / Bridgeman Images

ISBN 978-0-8308-4613-9 (print)
ISBN 978-0-8308-9946-3 (digital)

Printed in the United States of America ♾

 As a member of the Green Press Initiative, InterVarsity Press is committed to protecting the environment and to the responsible use of natural resources. To learn more, visit greenpressinitiative.org.

Library of Congress Cataloging-in-Publication Data
Benner, David G.
Desiring God's will : aligning our hearts with the heart of God / David G. Benner. -- Expanded Edition.
pages cm. -- (The spiritual journey)
Includes bibliographical references.
ISBN 978-0-8308-4613-9 (pbk. : alk. paper)
1. Submissiveness--Religious aspects--Christianity. 2. Will--Religious aspects--Christianity. 3. God (Christianity)--Worship and love. 4. Christian life. I. Title.
BV4647.A25B46 2015
248.4--dc23
2015022993

P 21 20 19 18 17 16 15 14 13 12 11 10 9 8 7 6 5 4 3

Y 33 32 31 30 29 28 27 26 25 24 23 22 21 20 19 18

To my father—Gordon Benner

and my brother—Colin Benner

who have both taught me much

about desiring God's will.

Contents

Foreword

by Thomas H. Green, SJ

S t. Ignatius Loyola, to whom David Benner refers frequently in this very helpful book, composed the first formal retreat in the church's history, the *Spiritual Exercises*, in the sixteenth century. His small manual contains the classic rules for discernment of the diverse spirits at work in our lives, that we may recognize and follow God's voice despite the many conflicting voices (the world, the flesh and the devil) that we hear.

While David Benner gives some basic introductory guidelines in his final chapter for the actual process of discerning, his real topic here is, as the title indicates, *desiring* God's will. Before we can discern we must be properly disposed to do so. In fact, the whole dynamic of Ignatius's exercises is to bring the retreatant to that open, listening attitude in which real discernment is possible.

David Benner, being both a psychologist and a spiritual director, has a unique perspective in assisting the contemporary pray-er to achieve that true openness which is essential for genuine discernment. As he explains, the real choice we all face is between "the

kingdom of God and the kingdom of self." He then explains the
many ways that we can become trapped in the kingdom of self, and
the many ways the choice of the kingdom of God is today coun-
tercultural. His numerous experiential examples, drawn both from
his own life and from the lives of those he has directed, give us
concrete insight into the challenges we ourselves may face.

Benner's sources are truly ecumenical, in the best sense of that
word. He cites many of the great masters of spirituality, past and
present. The book thus achieves a happy balance of tradition and
contemporary relevance, seen by recalling that St. Ignatius himself
begins his *Spiritual Exercises* (#23) with what is known as the Prin-
ciple and Foundation. He tells the retreatant that our only end is
"the glory of God and our own salvation." Everything else on the
face of the earth is, and must be used as, a means to that sole end.
Ignatius does not claim that this is an easy stance to achieve. The
whole of the retreat is to help the retreatant to come to that dispo-
sition. And that, I believe, is precisely what David Benner is pro-
claiming in contemporary language: the challenging call to choose
the kingdom of God rather than the kingdom of self.

Willing God's Way

*T*his is a book that I resisted writing for months. I thought I had written enough about willfulness and surrender. I wanted to move on to other topics. I started another book but was unhappy with where it was going, troubled in my spirit. It was clearly my agenda—the fruit of my willful planning and resolve. How discouraging it was to again be reminded of the strength of my lust for self-determination and control, my deeply ingrained preference for my will over God's will.

I wish I could write about things that I have finally and solidly learned, things that are once and for all behind me. But my experience—and, I believe, the truth about the spiritual journey in general—is that past challenges and struggles are never fully behind us in this life. The route for the transformational journey of Christian spirituality is never direct. Typically it involves revisiting territory through which we have already passed, and doing so over and over again!

Doing things "my way" comes naturally for all of us. Egocentricity and self-control are fundamental dynamics of the human soul. We know we are supposed to surrender to God's will and may genuinely want to, but most of us continue to face the almost irresistible tendency to assert our own will. We overhear Jesus' prayer in the garden of Gethsemane—"Not my will, but thine be done"— but have trouble honestly making it our own.

This book is an extension of ideas presented in the two previous books in this trilogy—*Surrender to Love* and *The Gift of Being Yourself*.[1] Surrendering to God's will makes little sense if we are not first convinced of the depths of God's love for us. But surrender is far from complete, and we have yet to unwrap the gift of our true-self-in-Christ until we are fully convinced of the absolute trust-worthiness of God's will. Learning to prefer God's way to ours and discovering our identity and fulfillment in God's kingdom way demands that we know Love, deeply and personally. Only then will it be possible to choose God with the totality of our being, not just our will.

The problem is that when we approach the task of choosing any-thing other than our own self and its immediate gratification, most of us automatically turn to willpower and resolve. Choosing God then becomes more a matter of grim determination than joyful sur-render—closer to deciding to cut back on eating enjoyable foods than to following our heart to the Source of abundant life.

Another problem is that when we think of God's will we nor-mally assume that the challenge is how to *know* it rather than how to *choose* it. The focus on God's will is thus misplaced—limited to points of major decisions. We fail to recognize that our problem is not so much knowing God's way as being utterly convinced that choosing God is choosing life.

While the choices we make can be very important in our spir-itual journey, we shall see in what follows that *how* we decide can often be as important as *what* we decide. Willpower, determination and discipline are not enough in Christ-following. The close inter-connection of will and desire means that if Christ is to have our will, he must first have our heart.

The starting point in aligning our heart and will with the heart and will of God is to understand the difference between our natural willfulness and the God-given gift of willingness. The first three chapters each explore one important facet of this difference. In chapter one we examine the dark side of willfulness and the downside of discipline. Chapter two then looks at the differences between the ways of choosing associated with the kingdom of self and the kingdom of God, while chapter three takes what we learn about life in the kingdom of God and explores how our willing and choosing are transformed when they are shaped by love.

The next three chapters examine what it means to choose God. Chapter four focuses on learning attentive openness to the God who is attentively open and present to us. In chapter five we examine how willing God's way involves the heart's desires, not simply the head's resolve, while chapter six explores the role of taking up our cross in our choosing of God. Finally, chapter seven draws these strands together by examining the process of discernment—not just in making major decisions but in the moment-by-moment flow of ordinary days.

Learning to desire God's will is not something we can accomplish by resolve and willpower. As we shall see, it occurs only when we live so close to God's heart that the rhythm of our own heartbeat comes to reflect the divine pulse. Then and only then will we be able to truly pray, "Thy kingdom come, thy will be done on earth as it is in heaven." Then and only then will this prayer be our deepest desire.

Perhaps you can identify with me as one who has begun to know something of the depth of God's love but still resists fully surrendering to it. Perhaps you, like me, find yourself trying to co-opt God to fit your plans rather than submitting both your plans and your planning to divine willing. Perhaps you also have occasionally experienced the freedom that comes from floating in the river of life that is God but still spend much of your time swimming against the current. And perhaps you too find the battle for control to be one of the most discouraging and persistently nagging conflicts in your spiritual warfare.

Jesus is the only person who has lived a life of total surrender to God's loving will. He alone knew the absolute freedom and fulfillment of floating in the river of life that is God. He alone can lead us to the release from enslavement to an autonomous will. He alone can lead us to the freedom and fullness of life that is in God. It is my prayer that you and I alike may learn to prefer his way over our way as we journey together in what follows.

Hamilton, Canada
Pentecost

one

Ways of Willing

Most books on God's will seem to assume something I no longer believe. They seem to assume that we choose God's will in much the same way as we choose to pursue New Year's resolutions. I think this is incorrect and am convinced that the spiritual consequences of this misunderstanding are serious.

Think for a moment about the process of making New Year's resolutions. First we become aware of some change we feel we should make—more exercise, more praying, less anger, less eating, more play or something along these lines. Then we determine to do the thing we are trying to choose, screwing up our determination and fortifying our resolve. In short, we choose things that are not naturally attractive by reliance on willpower. This, we assume, is just what willpower is for. It is what separates strong people from weak people, those with strength of character from those without.

Don't misunderstand me. Bolstering our determination in order to do important things is obviously crucial for living. And doing things that are not naturally attractive is essential if we are to live responsibly. But what a tragedy if we lump choosing God in with things that are not naturally attractive. Is it any wonder that the thought of surrendering to God's will evokes mixed feelings? Choosing God's dream for us feels like choosing to take bitter medicine.

Thankfully there are other ways of choosing that are less reliant on willpower and grim determination. These we will examine in later chapters. Before doing so, however, it is important to understand the limitations of our natural ways of choosing. For until we realize the dangers of willfulness we will not be ready to embrace the life-giving freedom of willing surrender.

THE DARK SIDE OF WILLFULNESS

I have always loved accounts of seafaring adventures—the challenge of men (and in some cases women) facing the worst that nature can hurl against them as they attempt to survive and reach their destination. They inspire me in my own modest efforts as a freshwater sailor, stimulating my desire to push the limits of boat and self but providing enough vicarious gratification that I'm able to leave the real risks to others.

Since I first read it as a child, Herman Melville's *Moby Dick* has been one of my favorites of this genre. Captain Ahab is among the great strong-willed characters of Western literature. I have always liked him. Although I wish it were not so, I must admit that I share some of his stubbornness. But even if you cannot identify with him, he commands notice as a striking example of willfulness run amuck.

Captain of the *Pequod,* a nineteenth-century whaling vessel sailing out of Nantucket, Ahab is a man with determination of steel. "Old Thunder"—as he is known by his crew—is unflinching in his resolve to hunt down and kill the whale that took his leg. Nothing can dent his resolve, not even the mutinous intentions of his crew. He will allow nothing to stand in his way. With brazen bravado he challenges the gods to try to stop him from following his plan:

You've knocked me down, and I'm up again, but ye have run and hidden. Come forth from behind your cotton bags! I have no long gun to reach ye. Come . . . and see if ye can swerve me. Swerve me? Ye cannot swerve me, else ye swerve yourselves! . . . The path to my fixed purpose is laid with iron rails, whereon my soul is grooved to run.[1]

Who is this man who makes his motto "What I've dared, I've willed; and what I've willed, I'll do!"?[2] He is every man and every woman—perhaps just a little more daring, a little more stubborn and a little more maniacally fixed on the ends of his choosing. He is willpower that is out of control. He shows us the dangers of willfulness when it is elevated to the status of the supreme good. He shows us the enslavement of a self-originating autonomous will that is unchecked by love.

My Way or No Way

In our choosing and willing, whether we recognize it or not, we all have a bit of Old Thunder within. In each of us there lives a two-year-old with clenched fists, gritted teeth and defiance blazing in his or her eyes. We differ only in terms of how much life this two-year-old still has and how she or he expresses that vigor.

You may have heard the story of the little boy—a bit older than two but still dominated by his inner two-year-old—who was running around the house in a fit of hyperactive frenzy. He was chasing the cat, jumping on the furniture, provoking his brother and driving his mother to distraction. Repeatedly she told him to stop running around and sit still. He refused. Finally, in exasperation—and with more volume and forcefulness than intended—she took him by the arm, sat him at her feet on the floor and told him not to move a muscle.

Crossing his arms, he looked up at her in defiance and said, "I may be sitting down on the outside, but I'm standing up on the inside!"

It is sometime between eighteen and thirty-six months of age that we normally first discover the seductive power of asserting our will. Most of us spend much of the rest of our life trying to relinquish it.

Willfulness depends on self-regulation, and self-regulation has its roots in the muscular control that usually develops in the second year of life. Anyone who has stooped to repeatedly retrieve treasured objects dropped by a high-chaired child knows that holding-on-and-letting-go is a game of endless enjoyment for youngsters. But it isn't just play. It's a laboratory for learning to choose, act and control. Bladder and bowel regulation is being learned around the same time. This is also the point at which the infant makes the first choices between *willfulness* as a weapon in the battle for control and *willingness*—what Erik Erikson describes as a relaxed decision "to let pass and let be."[3]

Learning to assert our will is essential for normal psychological development. It is a basic part of human agency—that is, the capacity to choose, act and live responsibly. One must *have* willful self-regulation before it can be surrendered. What we are witnessing as the young child first discovers the power of the will is the development of the self and the capacity for choice, determination and action—all things that are essential to basic life competence.

In adults we tend to think of willpower as an admirable asset. We praise the person who can stick to a diet or maintain an exercise plan or spiritual discipline. We admire the person who resists the temptation to passivity in the face of tough challenges that demand action. We respect the person who can set a personal agenda and stick to it. And we judge the person lacking in this stick-to-it-iveness to be lacking in character development.

But while the capacity to choose and follow through is essential for both psychological and spiritual maturity, willpower is easily overrated. It can have a much more malignant quality.

MALIGNANT WILLFULNESS

Think, for example, of Judas. Although his betrayal of Jesus has come to define his character, we must look deeper into his story in order to understand both this act and him.

Each of the first disciples responded to Jesus' call to follow him for different and complex reasons. But despite the limitations of psychological analysis from the distant vantage point of the twenty-first century, it seems safe to say that Judas did not initially agree to follow Jesus with the intent of betraying him. Something went badly wrong.

Like the others, Judas was undoubtedly very impressed with Jesus at first. Jesus was different from anyone he had ever encountered. He spoke with an authority that made it hard to ignore him (Matthew 7:29). Something about him made you either love him or hate him—want to follow him to the ends of the world or kill him. It was, and is, hard to find a middle ground of neutrality with Jesus. But Judas easily knew where he stood. He wanted to follow Jesus. He saw in him the possibility of the fulfillment of the deepest hopes of his people.

To be a first-century Jew in Palestine was to live with an unavoidable consciousness of living in an occupied country. Jews typically viewed their Roman invaders with some combination of smoldering resentment and hatred. They longed to be free of their oppression. For generations they had awaited the arrival of a Messiah who would deliver them from their enemies and lead them into a glorious future. For those in whom this hope had not yet died, the present seemed to be the perfect time for such deliverance.

Jesus undoubtedly mobilized the hopes and passions of Judas. Even before meeting him Judas appears to have been a man of

passion. Biblical scholars suggest that he may have been a member
of the radical, anti-Roman, Jewish nationalist group known as the
Zealots. At least one of the other disciples was identified with this
group—Simon (Matthew 10:4)—and it is easy to understand why
its members would have been strongly attracted to Jesus. Jesus
clearly held promise of being the hoped-for "King of the Jews."

It is probable that this hope became the focus of Judas Iscariot's
willfulness. Clearly, at some point the differences between his plan
for Jesus and God's plan became apparent. If he had not been stub-
bornly determined to pursue his own agenda, he could have traded
his disappointment in his plan for the deeper hope of the will of
God. This would have interrupted the spiral of death in which he
was caught by that point. But it was not to be.

The willful, stubborn pursuit of his own agenda was likely
behind his betrayal of Jesus. His hope appears to have been that
Jesus would be a political messiah and restore Jewish honor by
leading an insurrection against the Romans. If so, his betrayal of
Jesus to the Roman authorities may well have been a desperate
attempt to force Jesus to abandon his passivity. When confronted
with imminent arrest, he may have hoped Jesus would finally
shake off his lethargy and put his obvious talents into the service
of political liberation. Or Judas may simply have been acting out
of resentment that came from realizing that his plans for Jesus had
been frustrated.

The truth is that as a naked force of self-propulsion, willfulness is both spiritually and psychologically destructive. Not to
be confused with acting on the strength of conviction or following through on difficult things that need to be done, willfulness is stubbornness and rigidity. It is the irrational Captain
Ahab within us, gritting his teeth and refusing to let go and let
be. It's a grandiose, inflated self acting as if it is master and com-
mander of the universe.

Looked at carefully, willfulness is more *against* something than *for* something. My willful self refuses to quit as I seek to push through my writing block or finish lecture preparation even when my spirit is dry and my body is telling me to take a break. A spirit of willingness invites me to pause and turn to God, simply opening to God for a moment, letting God bring perspective and clarity about my need to stop writing for the night or throw out what I've started and wait for the gift of a fresh idea. Willfulness, in either circumstance, is my fight against quitting, against attending to my body, against attending to God's Spirit. The act of willing surrender is a choice of openness, a choice of abandonment of self-determination, a choice of cooperation with God.

The motto of willfulness is "My way or no way." Because of this, willfulness leads to death, not freedom. It is an act of rebellion— the residue of the unredeemed two-year-old who continues to sit in stubborn defiance in a dark corner of our soul, unwilling to let go and let be. In more distinctively Christian terms, it is the unwillingness to offer the prayer of release taught and modeled by our Lord: "Not my will, but thine be done."

Not Me

But let me pause for a moment in case you are having trouble connecting with this. Nobody wants to see himself or herself in Judas, and Captain Ahab may be a bit too extreme for easy identification. Perhaps you are not aware of the lurking presence of willfulness or even the presence of a strong-willed inner two-year-old. Possibly, therefore, you are doubting the danger of reliance on determination and discipline.

Your feelings are understandable. You may be thinking of the numerous biblical encouragements to discipline and perseverance or the central place the spiritual disciplines have played across the history of the Christian church.

In the service of valuable goals, discipline is unquestionably a good thing. Paul tells his readers, "Discipline yourself for the purpose of godliness" (1 Timothy 4:7 NASB), and the epistles are full of commands to action that require resolve and determination to implement. Discipline increases the chances that we will do the right things—that good intentions will be realized. It helps resolutions become habits. And it is clearly part of the process of transforming spiritual intentions into spiritual habits.

Discipline, spiritual or otherwise, is a good servant but a bad master. It is not the *summum bonum*—the supreme good. When it is valued in and of itself, the disciplined life easily leads to rigidity and pride. These are worth further consideration, because often they are the most easily identifiable markers of the presence of malignant willfulness.

RIGIDITY

The blade of grass that is supple and flexible is alive. The one that is brittle and stiff is either dead or dying. So it is in all of nature—humans included. Rigidity is a dynamic of death. And it is a blight that easily infects the vine of a highly disciplined life.

Consistent implementation of resolutions demands a high degree of self-control. But when self-control is overvalued and is not balanced by other "softer" virtues—particularly love—it leads to rigidity.

The danger of self-control is that it easily generalizes to control of one's total life space—including those who enter that space. I think of how easily I can feel uncomfortable around people who are much more spontaneous and free than I. Such people are hard to predict and hard to control. Consequently, they threaten the arbitrary controls I place on myself—the brittle barriers I erect around my naked self in an attempt to hide my vulnerability and make me feel safe.

Unchecked self-control sucks the vitality not only out of the individual who practices it but also out of others. In its most advanced stages it produces a rigidity that looks like premature rigor mortis. You can smell the presence of death when you are with someone who is in the embrace of the soul-damaging rigidity associated with self-control that has been made into the supreme virtue.

An elderly man in our church when I was growing up was recognized by us kids as someone who didn't like children. (Kids can just tell that sort of thing!) One Sunday he turned around in the midst of the service and blasted my brother and me for inadvertently kicking his seat. It would have been bad enough if he had done so discreetly. But being almost deaf, he spoke so loudly that the whole service was interrupted. I recall wishing the ground would open up and swallow me then and there. But it didn't.

After church my parents offered much-needed comfort. They also told us a bit about the man in the hope that admiration for him might help us be more forgiving. They told us how much he loved the Lord and how diligent he was in his "spiritual walk." He had memorized whole books of the Bible, and reportedly spent hours each day in prayer. He was, in short, supposed to be a model of Christian virtue—an exemplar of the life of spiritual discipline.

I saw no evidence, however, that his discipline was in the support of life—either his own or anyone else's. I saw only morbid levels of rigidity. I experienced only the shudder associated with the passing shadow of death.

Soul-damaging rigidity is seen in a stubborn, inflexible determination to live *my* life *my* way. It is seen in an inability to ever choose the unexpected, the spontaneous or the interruption—to ever simply go with the flow. Patterns and habits that may be good in general are now the obsessions and compulsions of a life of stifling overcontrol. This is saying yes to death, not life.

Jesus showed nothing of this rigidity. Although the strength of his resolve and consistency of his spiritual disciplines are striking, he lived a life characterized by flexibility, not predictability. He was constantly surprising people—always capable of spontaneously embracing the opportunities of the moment, never compulsively grasping the safety of the habitual. His discipline served to align his will and his spirit with God's will and God's Spirit. But this discipline was not dependent on external rigidity. It sprang from a heart that was aflame with the love of God, not a will that was striving for self-control.

PRIDE

Highly disciplined people are also prone to pride and a smug sense of superiority. They feel self-righteous because of their ability to commit themselves to a plan of action and then successfully implement it. They tend to view willpower as a singularly important virtue. And although their private attitudes may be well masked, they are prone to be judgmental of those they perceive to be lacking in this virtue.

One of the most highly disciplined people I have ever had the opportunity to know well was a man in his late thirties who consulted me about problems with anger. Because of his well-developed capacity for self-control, he incorrectly thought that no one other than his wife had any idea of this problem. He, however, was aware of its nagging presence and sought help to better manage his feelings.

Michael was a teacher in a nationally recognized private school. Held in high esteem by his students and recently selected teacher of the year by his colleagues, he gave every appearance of being very competent in his work. This appearance was very important to him, as was appearance in general. In fact, both were much more important than he could acknowledge.

Early in our work together Michael told me that his life motto was "Where there's a will, there's a way." He lived by discipline and determination and, like Captain Ahab, said that if he set his mind to something he never failed to succeed. This statement betrayed not just his arrogance but also his youth. Apart from his simmering anger, he said he had yet to encounter a situation where willpower, discipline and hard work had let him down.

Discipline characterized every aspect of his life. He was a highly competitive runner who ran—snow, rain or shine—four days a week for at least two hours each day. He was also fastidious in maintaining his spiritual disciplines of daily prayer and Bible reading, allocating from 5:10 to 5:30 each morning for his soul before heading off to take care of his body. The rest of his day was equally regimented—disciplined eating, disciplined work, disciplined in setting and keeping "appointments" with friends, disciplined in keeping up with his email and disciplined in his sleep patterns.

But all that discipline made him proud. He went through his day comparing himself to others, always with a favorable result. He felt enormous secret pride about extremely insignificant things. He confessed, for example, that he prided himself on being able to go to the bathroom less often than others. He also took a private delight in what he judged to be the superiority of his ability to judge the passage of time—periodically glancing at his watch throughout the day to test himself. It was irrelevant whether others knew that he could do these and other such trivial things. It was enough that *he* knew of them, as they were proof of his superiority over other mere mortals that lacked self-mastery.

Not surprisingly, Michael's secret pride was matched by an equally secret contempt for anyone who seemed to lack discipline. This included people who were overweight, disheveled in appearance, poor, inarticulate, lacking in intelligence or in any way lacking in competence and success. He knew these attitudes were not nice, and he was keenly aware that they were not Christian. But he kept them in check with the same ironclad resolve with which he ran his life and assumed they were thus of no real consequence. His attitudes were not as secret as he thought. His private contempt bled through in indirect ways that were obvious to others.

Pride alienates us from others. It also spawns an illusory sense of self-sufficiency. Michael was convinced that his willpower was strong enough to let him master life, including any difficult circumstance he might face. He didn't need anybody. He liked certain people and chose to spend time with them. But he prided himself on not needing them.

Psychologically, Michael's willpower served as a defense against his deep longings for intimacy and dependence. His reliance on himself was an exaggerated expression of the opposite of what he was really desiring and feeling. Under his bluster of independence and self-sufficiency was a little boy who longed for someone to take care of him. He desperately wanted to give up having to be so competent. He wanted to need someone, not simply have others need him.

Willfulness was the shield behind which Michael hid his fear of being out of control. Pride and rigidity were the chain-mail armor with which he sought to protect himself from vulnerability. Eventually he was able to lower this defense and begin to experience true life. But this did not happen until his will was softened by love—not until he dared to meet God in nakedness and not until he learned to meet others in genuine openness and vulnerability.

LIFE-ENHANCING DISCIPLINE

Don't misunderstand what I am saying. Discipline does not automatically lead to either rigidity or pride. But when discipline, willpower and self-control are overvalued and when they become the goal—not merely the means to good ends—vitality and well-being are sapped from our soul.

Self-discipline can enhance vitality. Proverbs 4:13 encourages us to "hold fast to discipline, never let her go, keep your eyes on her, she is your life." This was clearly true of Jesus. His embrace of discipline was an embrace of life. When he headed to the Mount of Olives early each morning for prayer (Luke 22:39-41), he was not building an image, earning spiritual points with God or demonstrating to himself that he could follow through with a commitment. He was following his heart. He longed to be with his Father because this relationship was the source of his life. Discipline was, for Jesus as it should be for us, grounded in relationship and shaped by desire.

Spiritual disciplines should always be means to spiritual ends, never ends in themselves. They are places of meeting God that do not have value in and of themselves. To treat them as if they did is to develop a spirituality that is external, self-energized and legalistic.

Genuine Christian spirituality places the priority on inner transformation, not outward routines. Changed behavior should flow out of a changed heart, not simply a strong will. Spiritual disciplines should be what Kenneth Boa describes as "external practices that reflect and reinforce internal aspirations,"[4] not simply the fruit of willpower. They are "the product of a synergy between divine and human initiative ... [serving] as a means of grace insofar as they bring our personalities under the lordship of Christ and the control of the Spirit."[5]

Jesus told his disciples that he came to give life—abundant, extravagant, overflowing life that would result from the indwelling presence of the Spirit of God. Speaking to the Samaritan woman at the well, he told her that anyone who drank the water he was prepared to give would never be thirsty again, because it would turn into an inner spring of everlasting life (John 4:14).

How tragic that our discipline—spiritual or otherwise—sometimes chokes off that vitality. How dangerous when we feel a smug (even if very private), idolatrous pride in our capacity for willfulness, resolve and self-determination—even in good things like prayer, Bible reading or Christian service.

The life Jesus came to bring is a life that does not depend on willpower. It flows out of the Spirit of God, energizing and transforming our spirit. It's a life based on transfusion—God's Spirit transfusing my spirit, God's deepest desires, longings and dreams becoming mine. This is the way—and the only way—to the freedom and fulfillment of preferring God's will to mine.

Most of the time my stubborn inner two-year-old is relatively well hidden. I no longer stomp off and refuse to participate if a situation doesn't go the way I want it to go—or at least I don't do this as often or obviously as I did as a strong-willed child! I don't stamp my feet and clench my fists as I spit out "No!" in response to anything I dislike. I have learned to be more subtle in my willfulness. But I am still easily caught up in "my way or no way." And paradoxically, it most frequently occurs in terms of my reluctance to surrender to God's will.

Living life "our way" appears to be the hardwired default option for all of us. It just comes naturally. We instinctively know how to do it. And often—at least in the short term—it seems to work reasonably well.

Before proceeding, take a few moments to prayerfully reflect on the patterns of your own willfulness. Dialogue with God about the motivations behind your discipline—especially your spiritual disciplines. Consider whether you, like me, can identify with Judas in his desire to co-opt God to fit into his own plans. Or possibly you can relate to his craftiness in disguising the fact that he remained captain of his own soul while appearing to have surrendered his allegiance to Christ.

This chapter has presented the dark side of the will. In chapter three we will present the antidote—love. There we will see that rigidity and pride fade away when our willing is shaped by love. But before we turn to this, we need to understand the radical difference between the kingdom of self and the kingdom of God. Willfulness is the deadly fruit of the kingdom of self. Willingness is the river of life flowing through the kingdom of God.

two

My Kingdom, Thy Kingdom

Wh 	hen it comes right down to it, there are really only two possible prayers that can be prayed. One is entirely natural, one is absolutely supernatural. Whether we choose to pray or not, one of these will be praying itself. The choice is not whether to pray. The choice is which prayer to pray.

The prayer that comes most naturally for all of us is, "My name be hallowed, my kingdom come, my will be done." This is a prayer of independence and willfulness. It is the liturgy of the kingdom of self. The prayer that goes against our nature and that can become our prayer only through the action of divine grace is the Lord's Prayer. It inverts everything in the liturgy of the kingdom of the self—"thy name be hallowed, thy kingdom come, thy will be done." It is a prayer of surrendered autonomy and willingness. It is the liturgy of the kingdom of God.

> Our Father who art in heaven,
> hallowed be thy name.
> Thy kingdom come,
> thy will be done on earth as it is in heaven.
> Give us this day our daily bread,

and forgive us our trespasses
as we forgive those who trespass against us.
And lead us not into temptation,
but deliver us from evil.
For thine is the kingdom and the power
and the glory for ever and ever.
Amen.

Although many of us repeat or sing the words of the super-natural prayer of God's kingdom each time we are in church (and millions say it daily), much of the time we are guilty of not really praying it. If we honestly thought about what we were praying, we would have to quickly stop our mouth. It is a subversive prayer. It requests that life as we know it be overturned. To truly pray this prayer is to choose death for the kingdom of self. It's a choice to take up our cross and follow Jesus.

But in order to truly make this prayer ours, we must start at the beginning—where our Lord starts. Although we tend to rush over the first words, it is here that we discover the first hints of the possibility of the surrender of our will.

OUR FATHER

I really discovered this prayer only when I moved it from its liturgical context as a part of corporate worship and began to make it part of my personal daily prayer. What immediately struck me was that it didn't begin the way I normally begin my prayers. It didn't begin with *my, me* or *I.*

The first word forced me to notice that the prayer our Lord offers as the model for Christian prayer brings me into God's presence in the company of others. Who are these other people with whom I name the name of the Father? Together we approach God, and together we ask that the divine name be hallowed and the kingdom of God come. Together we ask for *our* daily bread, together we ask for the forgiveness of *our* sins, and together we choose his will over *our* will.

Louis Evely, a Belgian priest whose writings on spiritual life are popular in Europe, suggests that in order to be sons and daughters of God we must be brothers and sisters to God's other children.[1] God willed community because God is community. God exists in relationship. "He needed to be several to be love."[2] We come to this God who is a community of love in the company of Jesus and all who call God Father. We are led by Jesus, who teaches us what it is to truly relate to our Father God and to our brothers and sisters (1 John 1:3-4).

The reason the Lord gave us an "our Father" rather than "my Father" prayer is that the God who is a community of love wants to expand that community of love. That is simply the nature of love, the nature of God. Evely writes, "God is effusion. All men have been made in the image of God. We cannot be Father all on our own. We cannot be Son all on our own. We cannot be Spirit of exchange and love all on our own."[3] If we ceased to be brothers and sisters to the other children of God, if we really were separate beings, we would be in the image of a lonely god that is definitely not the Christian God.

Beginning prayer with "our" rather than "my" takes the focus off me. The natural tendency, of course, is to see God through the filter of my needs, my desires, my kingdom, my will. But the god we encounter in such prayer is—at best—only a shadow of the Christian God. The god we encounter when we fail to get beyond our self is the god of our wishes and projections, a god seriously lacking in transcendence.

The Father God to whom Jesus points is altogether different from any god we could have ever imagined. Far from being a projection of our longings onto the cosmos (as envisaged by Freud), the Christian God reaches across the chasm that separates the divine from the human and reveals God to be the Father after whom all mothers and fathers take their name. This is the God whose name is Love, not simply a god who is loving. This is a God who wants to give us the divine love nature.

To truly receive Love—to become love—we must be prepared to surrender the keys to the kingdom of self. Intuitively we believe the lie that the route to personal freedom and fulfillment is through self-assertion and self-determination—through grasping and control. The way that has its roots in the nature of the Father God whose name is Love is totally different. We become love only by surrender and self-sacrifice. The beginning of this journey is the return to "our Father," a journey that we take with the other prodigal sons and daughters who are our brothers and sisters.

The God we address as "our Father" is the God who freely gives the one thing that can release us from the tyranny of self-assertion and an autonomous ego: perfect love. In this prayer that points the way from the kingdom of self to the kingdom of God we meet the God who desires nothing more than to expand the circle of love that is the fellowship of the Godhead. This is the God who at the end of time will say to those who come to God as "our Father," "I will be their God, and they shall be sons and daughters to me" (see Revelation 21:7).

THY KINGDOM COME

The first thing we cannot help but notice when we encounter "our Father" is how wholly *other* God is. This is what it means when we pray "who art in heaven." We ask that God's name be hallowed not because God is distant or powerful but because God is majestic and awesome. We will never come to prefer God's kingdom and will to ours until we meet the Divine in this relationship of love intermixed with wonder. But it must be a wonder that recognizes, as Simone Weil says, that the one thing we can know about God with the most certainty is that God "is what we are not."[4]

There would be no reason to submit our will to a tame god of our imagination. No god that is merely a projection of our deepest needs and longings is worthy of surrender of our soul. Surrendering to God's will begins by encountering God's grandeur. It also involves falling in love with God's grand plan of restoration of all things. This lies at the heart of God's will and God's kingdom.

Apart from duress and fear, nobody voluntarily submits their will and surrenders their autonomy for any other reason than love. But the only love that is powerful enough to make us *want* to turn over the keys of the kingdom of self, not simply *willing* to do so, is the love of God that springs from a deep personal knowing of God's love for us. This love grows out of an understanding of the divine kingdom plan—because to really understand this plan is to make us want to be part of the cosmic society the kingdom of love represents!

One of the suggested meditations in the Ignatian spiritual exercises is what St. Ignatius called the "kingdom exercise."[5] Take a moment and allow yourself to experience it.

Imagine meeting someone whom you immediately recognize to be a man or woman of outstanding intelligence, deep compassion, astounding competence and unquestionable trustworthiness. Others also recognize these qualities, and this person quickly gathers a following. Imagine him or her offering you the following call: "My work is to overcome all injustice, all poverty and all disease. I want you to join me in this. If you do, however, you must be prepared to devote your whole life to our cause, so that afterward you may share with me and many others in our victory." How inviting and compelling such a call would be!

But now consider Jesus and his call. If a cause espoused by a human being can have such appeal, how much greater is the attraction of the cause championed by Jesus! His call again comes to

you, just as personally—but it also goes out to the entire human
race: "I am come to inaugurate the kingdom of God and bring a
reign of love to the world. I will conquer everything that afflicts
you and the world—disease, sin, suffering, injustice, poverty, igno-
rance and even death. Come and join me so that I may first lead
you to the Father's healing love and saving grace. Then take up your
place beside me—sharing my labor, sharing my suffering and
sharing the victory that is certain." With God offering the invitation and the outcome assured, how can I resist a wholehearted
giving of self to Jesus and the cause of God's kingdom?

I had been a Christ-follower for many years when I spent a week
meditating on this simple exercise and the passages associated with
the launch of Christ's public ministry. It changed my Christ-
following. It propelled me from obedience to surrender. It stirred
my idealism and made me excited to reaffirm my allegiance to
Christ's call. It renewed my love for Jesus and gave fresh energy to
my sense of what an honor it is to be a Christian. It brought into
focus the enormity of the cause with which I was aligning myself
as I took the name of Christ and stood beside him addressing "our
Father." It gave me new levels of passion in my work and prayer for
the coming of God's kingdom. It made me genuinely excited to be
able to be a part of God's plan to "bring everything together under
Christ, as head, everything in the heavens and everything on earth"
(Ephesians 1:10).

Origen, the third-century church father, reminds us that in surrendering our will to Christ "we become one spirit with him, and
thereby accomplish his will, in such wise that it will be perfect on
earth as in heaven."[6] Our assent to God's will is the means of our
participation in God's cosmic restoration agenda through his
reign of love.

God loves so much that he wants to transform all people and all
things by love. God wants to spread love by propagating the divine

self in us and through us. This is the nature of God's love and the work of God's kingdom. The hope of this kingdom is the assurance that Love will prevail. Our confidence in this certainty is based on God's Word: "I have conquered the world" (John 16:33). The kingdom of God will prevail! Hallelujah!

THY WILL BE DONE

God's will cannot be separated from God's kingdom. Establishing the divine reign of love on earth is God's big plan. The smaller details of divine will all fit within this.

This is the wisdom of the Lord's Prayer as it teaches us to first see the nature of the Father, then grasp the grandeur of God's kingdom, and only then feel within us the desire to get on board by surrendering our will. Once we truly encounter Perfect Love and the kingdom plan to make this love the rule not only of heaven but also of earth, surrender is less an act of volition than an impulse of love.

Our ambivalence about surrender to God is based on the illusory security of the kingdom of self in relation to the apparent risk of the kingdom of God. God terrifies humans. In the words of Louis Evely, "He is total self-denial. He is entirely directed toward another.... He knows no rest, no satisfaction, no withdrawal within himself."[7] We, on the other hand, have a deeply ingrained tendency to rely on ourselves. We want love without sacrifice—without the risk and expense of the surrender of self-control and determination. God cannot accept such a bargain.

Finding our self by first losing our self simply seems too risky for most of us. We want to make a bargain with God. Surely any reasonable god would recognize that something is better than nothing and allow us to continue to play our game of trying to do our own will while fitting as much as possible of God's will within it. It seems like such a reasonable first step toward complete surrender.

But our game is fatal. For while pretending to put ourselves in a place where we can be transformed by Love, we actually remain in love only with our autonomous and willful self. And the kingdom of self is ultimately the kingdom of death.

We have believed the lie of the serpent. We have believed that freedom comes from the exercise of our autonomy. But true autonomy lies in the choice to give ourselves to others in love. It lies in the absolute surrender of our self to God and the kingdom of love. The paradoxical law of God's kingdom is that it is only when we give up what we clutch most desperately that we will receive it. Grasping destroys. Surrender restores and transforms.

Don't fool yourself about how difficult surrender to God—preferring God's will to our own—really is. I mentioned the value I found in making the Lord's Prayer part of my daily personal prayer. It was, in fact, much more than a part. For over a year I stayed with a meditative offering of this prayer daily, choosing to not leave this incredibly powerful prayer and return to prayers of my own construction until I had plumbed its depths and truly made it mine. Daily I would pray a phrase and then allow the Spirit to speak to me and through me as I allowed that phrase to wash around inside my spirit. But daily I would feel one phrase stick in my throat—"thy will be done." It was one thing to pray that God's will be done on earth as it is in heaven. It was another to intentionally ask that God's will—not mine—be done in my life that day.

When I finally was able to talk with God about this difficulty, not simply try to ignore it, I began to notice a shift in my response to the prayer. I asked God to help me make this my prayer, my deepest desire. And slowly I found God beginning to answer this request. I began to discover longing, not simply guilt, when I came to that phrase. I began to experience God's heart and God's desire within me.

There is no reason to feel guilty if you find it difficult to surrender to God's will. Even Christ found it hard. He who knew the depth and dependability of the love of God better than any human also struggled to surrender to the demand of Love that he lay down his life. It seemed to be—and was—horribly unnatural. It took Jesus a whole night of agony before he could say, "Thy will be done" (Matthew 26:36-46). With distress and sorrow "unto death" (Matthew 26:38), Jesus first begged God to release him from the obligation of divine will.

But this was not his deepest desire, not his most fundamental prayer. More than anything in the world he wanted to know the intimate communion of love that was his relationship with the Father. His deepest wish was "Nevertheless, let it be as you, not I, would have it" (Matthew 26:39).

THE FREEDOM OF SURRENDER

After Jesus, there is no better biblical example of this surrender than Mary, his mother. As a young woman, Mary obviously had her own plans for her life. She probably had marriage and children in mind. But it was definitely not the kind of family God proposed!

Among the many reasons Christians honor Mary is the fact that as the first Christian—the first to accept Jesus within her—she models perfect surrender. "Mary was the first to accept that redemption should take place in the way we do not want it to take place; ruining all our plans, all our expectations, causing them to fail."[8] Mary agreed to allow God to deprive her of the one thing we count most basic among our natural rights—the right of self-control. Mary simply trusted that God knew best. With only one basic biological question ("How can these things be?") and without argument, she placed her trust in God. Her response to the shocking news delivered by the angel: "I am the handmaid of the Lord; . . . let what you have said be done to me" (Luke 1:38).

The demands on Mary's trust in God did not end at the annunciation. It got even worse. For the first thirty years, the grand promises made to Mary seemed to be unfulfilled. There were only the vaguest of signs that this son by such mysterious means was destined to reign over the house of Jacob forever as the Son of the Most High (Luke 1:32-33). Only her absolute trust in God could equip her to receive the rebuff that Jesus seemed to offer her on several occasions (John 2:4; Luke 8:20-21). At every point, even standing at the foot of his cross and giving her son back to God, Mary freely offered her unequivocal consent to God's will. Her constant life posture: "I am the handmaid of the Lord; let what you have said be done."

God does not ask for resignation based on acquiescence in the absence of a better option. Nor does God ask for reluctant, grudging submission. What God wants is surrender based on love and trust. This is what we see in the life of Jesus. And it is what we see in the life of his mother, Mary—the woman whom the Bible describes as "most highly favored" because she dared to trust the promise that God was with her and for her (Luke 1:28).

THE TWO KINGDOMS

As the prayer of our Lord proceeds, it has even more to teach us about surrender. We learn that what God wants is that we (not I) come for our (not my) daily (not weekly) bread from him (not from the labor of my hands). How humiliating to have to turn up with others to find a provision for one day, and then return the next to hope to find the same!

Most of us so excel at ensuring our own ongoing supply of life's provisions that we find the idea of having to come back for daily bread offensive. But God invites us to abandon our neurotic displays of self-sufficiency. He invites us to surrender our stolen independence and exchange it for a willingly accepted dependence. God takes our humble offering of powerlessness and turns it into a voluntary subordination—a freely chosen laying down of our life that leads to our transformation and fulfillment.

Dallas Willard notes that although we may not feel particularly powerful, every one of us has a personal kingdom—or queendom—over which we reign. Our kingdom is "the range of our effective will. Whatever we genuinely have the say over is in our kingdom."[9] I know people who feel they have no power over anything in their world other than what they eat. They starve themselves as a way of exercising power in that limited sphere. I know others who feel all they have control over is their emotional expression. Hence they exercise that control with a reign no less magisterial than that of any monarch. Our kingdom of self may be big or small, but it will be the sphere within which we live and die until we dare to step outside it and embrace the kingdom of God with all our passion.

Ruled by the King of Love, the kingdom of God has a wholly different character from the kingdom of self. Consider the differences.

The Kingdom of Self	The Kingdom of God
• Ruled by self-interest	• Ruled by love
• Grasping	• Releasing
• Achievement	• Gift
• Effort	• Consent
• Independence	• Interdependence
• Holding	• Releasing
• Willful	• Willing
• Clenched fists and closed heart	• Open hands and heart
• Hard and brittle	• Soft and malleable
• Determination	• Transformation

When I imaginatively reflect on the kingdom of self, I see a dark room. In a corner is an embittered old man, hunched over from a lifetime of grasping and clutching. I also notice a musty scent—a whiff of death. Everything vital has long ago left this room, and all that remains is rapidly rotting.

My imaginative response to the kingdom of God is dramatically different. I let out the breath I was holding. Lightness of being flows through my body, and freshness and vitality fill me. I feel free. I feel alive.

Your personal associations with these two kingdoms may be quite different from mine. But if you take a moment to allow yourself to notice them, I suspect that they will reveal equally contrasting personal pictures and reactions.

Given the sharpness of the contrast, one might wonder how these two kingdoms can coexist. But they do. Many of us—perhaps even most of us—have one foot uncomfortably but firmly planted in each. Jesus warned about the dangers of trying to do this (Matthew 6:24). But fear, laziness, greed, mistrust and an illusory sense that ultimately we are in the best position to know how to achieve our own fulfillment keep us from an unequivocal surrender of the keys to the kingdom of self. Perhaps like Ananias and Sapphira (Acts 5:1-3) we foolishly make a pretense of turning over the keys but keep back an extra set just in case we need to take control again at some point in the future. In one way or another we try to keep our options open.

If I am honest, I have to admit that much of the time I find myself moving back and forth between the two kingdoms. I open my hands and heart to God and others, and then I find myself grasping and controlling life with clench-fisted willfulness. I catch sight of the grandeur of God's kingdom vision and feel the paltry worthlessness of my own, and then I find I have again turned from God and am busy protecting my petty self-interests and controlling my life to maximize what I think will be my fulfillment.

But after four decades of Christ-following, one thing above all has become supremely clear to me. *I can't make the spiritual changes that I want on my own.* I cannot will myself into surrender. I cannot simply screw up my determination and choose God's will over mine once and for all.

What I can do, however, is talk with God honestly about the realities of my soul. And I can turn back toward God and once again hear Jesus' gentle words of invitation:

> Come to me, all you who labor and are overburdened, and I will give you rest. Shoulder my yoke and learn from me, for I am gentle and humble in heart, and you will find rest for your souls. (Matthew 11:28-29)

Hearing this invitation, everything within me wants to draw near and receive the gift of love that Jesus represents—not out of obligation but out of a soul-aching desire. And each time I do, my heart is slowly but progressively more aligned with the heart of God—God's desires becoming my desires and God's will becoming my will.

Before proceeding to the next chapter, take some time to prayerfully reflect on the ways you continue to live in the kingdom of self and resist surrender to the reign of Perfect Love. Think about how you spend your money and use your time. Reflect on your dreams for yourself and others. What do these things tell you about which kingdom has your heart and primary allegiance?

As you do this, don't allow yourself to be distracted by feelings of guilt. They simply point you back toward yourself, typically leaving you still stuck but now more miserable. Guilt is not enough to motivate surrender.

Instead, ask for God's desires and priorities to become yours. Listen to the invitation of Jesus to join him in the reign of love that is life in the kingdom of God. Hear his call to come to him for the rest that results from taking up his cross and his cause. Ask him for fresh appreciation and renewed (or first-time) excitement about the possibility of working with him on the advancement of God's plan to displace all kingdoms of this world and replace them with his glorious reign. As Willard puts it: "Review your plans for living and base your life on this remarkable new opportunity."[10]

Kingdom of love

- willfulness → willingness
- softens will
- tempers all things
- w/o life is a cacophony
- w/o life is enslaved
- connects us to others &
  to life
- life or death

three

Love and Will

*I*t is now time to return to the question of the transformation of the will that we left at the close of chapter one. Recalling the potential dangers of a reliance on willpower that we examined there, we now face the question of how we can will without rigidity and pride. The answer lies in the nature of the kingdom of God.

As I have noted, the kingdom of God is the kingdom of love. It is love that transforms willfulness into willingness. It is love that softens will and brings it back to the service of life. Love tempers all things, transforms all things. Without love, life is a cacophony of booming gongs and clashing cymbals (1 Corinthians 13:1). Without love, we become as brittle as dead grass. Without love, personality becomes turned in upon itself and is enslaved.

In a classic discussion of love and will, Rollo May notes that without love, willpower is often little more than a twisted, self-centered demonstration of one's own character.[1] It points toward itself. It does not serve the higher purposes of connecting us to others and to life. And that which does not lead to life leads to death. There is no middle ground.

Think again of Michael, whose story I told in chapter one—the ridiculously disciplined teacher who was consumed by pride over such trivial private accomplishments as controlling his bladder for long periods or being able to accurately judge the passage of time. Michael's willful self-control did not enhance the vitality of his life. Instead it kept him focused on himself. But not only did it cut him off from others, it cut him off from the truth of his own self. Like a leaf torn from the branch, he was cut off from life and slowly sliding toward spiritual death.

but he was selfish

What Michael lacked was any meaningful surrender to love. He was married and said he loved his wife, and he was a Christian and claimed to love God. But love had not softened his soul. It was absent as a counterbalance to his determination and discipline. What a lover he would have made if he had turned his determination toward the purpose of enhancing the joy of a loved one! But both his will and his love were turned back on himself. All he really loved was his willpower and discipline.

Without love, will becomes mechanical and loses its spontaneity. Without love, will becomes rationalistic and moralistic. Without love, will replaces imagination with industry. Without love, will makes us boringly predictable and devoid of vitality.

Discipline and self-control hold out an illusory promise of making us the master of our fate and captain of our soul. But the perils of being an unconquerable soul are immense. As May notes, "If my soul is really unconquerable, I shall never fully love; for it is the nature of love to conquer all fortresses. And if I must cling to being the master of my fate, I shall never be able to let myself go in passion."[2]

Describing the limitations of the will, psychoanalyst Leslie Farber notes, "I can will knowledge, but not wisdom; going to bed, but not sleeping; meekness, but not humility; scrupulosity, but not virtue; self-assertion or bravado, but not courage; lust, but not love; commiseration, but not sympathy; congratulations, but not admiration; religiosity, but not faith."[3]

excessive religious activities

Ultimately, will cannot genuinely connect us to life. We cannot will love. But we can be open to love. We cannot will forgiveness. But we can be open to receiving the gift of a heart that is willing to forgive. We cannot will intimacy with God. But we can be open to an experiential knowing of God that comes as a divine gift of soul-satisfying spiritual friendship.

LOVE-SHAPED WILLING

A reliance on willpower blocks love until will learns to surrender to love. Unless our will is softened by love, it strangles life. Until our spiritual disciplines are motivated by love of God, they will block love of God. Unless our personal disciplines are shaped by our love of others, they feed our narcissism.

Will that is formed under the influence of love looks altogether different from will that is self-originating and self-controlled. Think again of Jesus. What motivated his spiritual discipline? Why, for example, did he regularly slip off to the mountains or the desert for prayer (Matthew 14:23; Luke 5:15-16)? And what was behind his fasting (Luke 4:2)? These holy habits show nothing of the will-fulness of a spiritual self-improvement plan. Jesus wasn't trying to make a statement or fulfill a personal commitment. In fact, I suspect these habits only look like discipline on the outside. The inner impulse for Jesus was something quite different.

The motive behind everything that Jesus did was love of God and a desire to know and fulfill his Father's will. Jesus' spiritual disciplines were meaningful only in light of the primacy of his relationship with the Father. They were vehicles of communion, venues of intimacy.

We see this first in Jesus' puzzled question to Mary and Joseph when they found him as a twelve-year-old talking with the teachers in the temple: "Why were you looking for me?" he asked with seeming surprise. "Did you not know that I must be busy with my

Father's affairs?" (Luke 2:49). This is echoed in his assertion that the one who does the will of his Father is his brother or sister (Matthew 12:50). Obedience was a family matter for Jesus. It was all about relationship. It was an act of love.

Love and will were never separate for Jesus. Love was the motive for his obedience of God (John 14:31), as he urged it be behind ours (John 14:23). He delighted to do God's will and in so doing epitomized the way fulfillment comes from surrender to perfect love. He was also the perfect expression of the way God's love comes to fulfillment in the person who wills and does God's will (1 John 2:3-5).

Only love was capable of empowering Jesus to choose God's will over his own when faced with the agony of death. This is what Paul was referring to when he urged the Christians in Ephesus to do the will of God *from the heart* (Ephesians 6:6 NIV). Spiritual disciplines that emerge simply as acts of the will are likely to be self-serving and legalistic. What God desires is external actions that spring from inner longings for relationship and intimacy, for this is his desire for us. This was what the Father found in the heart of Jesus. And it is the motive for spiritual willing that we can find in our life in Jesus as we follow him and live in his Spirit.

It is this love-shaped willing that is celebrated in the hymn of praise for divine law that we know as Psalm 119. Over and over again the psalmist declares his delight in doing God's will. He speaks of deep love for God's commands (v. 47), not merely willful compliance with them. In fact, God's will is valued more highly than the purest gold (v. 127) because it brings joy beyond all wealth (v. 14). Jesus was the perfect fulfillment of this union of love and will.

Love-shaped willing has a softness that teeth-gritting determination and discipline can never mimic. Love opens us up and makes us more alive, whereas determination makes us more closed and less vital. God wants to touch our heart with love, for if we genuinely allow divine access to our depths, obedience will flow

difference bt.
acting & doing
& believing

out of us like water from an inner spring. This is discipline turned
on its head—not the result of our effort but the fruit of God's
action in us.

WILLINGNESS AS CONSENT

Willfulness is living a stubborn *no*. Willingness is living a loving *yes*.

Willfulness is always a stand against something. What we
oppose may be something worth resisting. But being against things
has an impact on our soul that is quite different from the soul-
nourishing effect of being *for* things.

Something in me thrives under conditions of physical adversity
or challenge. Unfortunately, it is my willfulness. I quickly discover
the Captain Ahab in me when faced with circumstances that
suggest that I should quit. My determination in the face of these
obstacles is the fruit of a teeth-gritting no. I push on through the
pain or hardship because I refuse to quit. I will settle for nothing
less than completion of whatever course I have set. I am a very bad
person to be with on a hike if the weather turns sour and everyone
is feeling tired and grumpy and wants to rest. By that point my
willful *no* will be in fine form as I resist quitting and thrive in
dogged determination to push ahead.

A good deal of the same willful determination has been evident
in my spiritual life. For decades I dutifully spent a committed
period of time each day in prayer and Bible reading. Clearly I was
doing the right thing. But I was doing it for the wrong reasons. My
discipline was a no to quitting, a no to failure, a no to a casual
embrace of my Christian commitments. It was not a yes to an
encounter with God.

In contrast, I have begun to learn the love-shaped willingness of
making space for God in my day. No longer is there any grim-faced
determination in this. It is a choice that is motivated by love. Scriptures are a way to meet God, not to meet an obligation. Prayer is

not the fruit of my willfulness but the response of my heart to Love.

Obviously we sometimes need to start holy habits with determination. But we should never be content with staying there. The challenge is to allow our spiritual disciplines to become the fruit of love and desire, not merely guilt and obligation.

The same is true of other disciplines. What a difference there is between acts of kindness or mere human decency that I offer as a fruit of love and those I offer out of guilt-shaped determination. It may be better to do the right thing for the wrong reason than not to do it at all, but how dangerous it is to be content with behavior arising from motives that are lacking in love.

So what should I do when I think of a friend whom I feel I "should" contact because he is having a difficult time and needs my support? Rather than simply reacting to this "should," what I now attempt to do is take a moment to pray for my friend. Suddenly seeing him through God's eyes changes my obligation to an opportunity. Or it may suggest that what I should do is *not* visit. In either case, God's perspective changes my perspective and my motivation. It transforms my willing and doing, making them acts of consent.

This consent is really nothing more than allowing God's love to soften my heart. Love, and love alone, has the capacity to turn our willfulness into willingness. Any love has *some* potential to do so. Perfect love has the unique potential to do so perfectly and completely.

Living with Consent

We have looked to Jesus as the absolutely perfect example of surrendered willfulness. We saw him preferring the will of the Father to his own, even in the face of his agonizing desire to do otherwise. We saw the same trust and willingness in Mary, his mother, at the annunciation and throughout her life. But the holy family gives us one more remarkable example of submission to God's will: Joseph, the father of Jesus.[4]

Joseph is easily overlooked. He easily recedes into the background of the story of Jesus' life. That may be in part because of the focus of the Gospel narratives. But I am convinced it also tells us some very important things about Joseph.

Joseph was a man who was <u>willing</u> to allow God to interrupt his life. Like Mary, he had a life and he had plans for his future. Mary was part of that plan. Engaged to be married, he was filled with the hopes and dreams that anyone has at such a point of life. Finding his fiancée pregnant by somebody else was certainly <u>not</u> part of that dream!

Joseph's submissive openness to God's will is every bit as astounding as Mary's. However painful the discovery of her pregnancy must have been, his love for Mary made it impossible for him to pursue the obvious solution of saving his reputation by quickly and publicly denouncing her. Instead he decided that the way to deal with the disastrous situation they both faced was a secret dissolution of their relationship. At least this would save Mary's reputation if not rescue her from her dilemma.

But God's plan was something quite different. Matthew tells us after Joseph had made up his mind what he should do, an angel of the Lord appeared to him in a dream and said, "Joseph son of David, do not be afraid to take Mary home as your wife, because she has conceived what is in her by the Holy Spirit" (Matthew 1:20). His response illustrates the <u>simplicity and freedom of a life of consent</u>: "When Joseph woke up he did what the angel of the Lord had told him to do" (Matthew 1:24).

We don't know how Joseph learned to have such confidence in the goodness of God's will. Scriptures are silent on his past experience of God, as they are on what must have been his inner struggle at this revelation. But they make the important point: Joseph was attentive to God (not failing to hear God's word even in a dream) and open to God (immediately doing what God asked).

Joseph willingly accepted God's right to invade his life and turn it
upside down.

This trust was soon to be tested even further. Not long after the
birth of Jesus, Joseph was again visited by another angel in his dreams.
(One might have understood if he had developed a sleep disorder to
avoid further dreams!) This time he was told to get up, take the child
and his mother, and flee to Egypt to escape the wrath of Herod, who
sought to kill Jesus. And again Joseph immediately did what he was
told—leaving for Egypt that same night (Matthew 2:14).

Joseph lived a life of consent to God's will. He was willing to
put God's plan for his life ahead of his own. God captured Joseph's
attention, and he remained attuned and receptive, ever attentive to
where God was in his life and where he was being led.

Chosen by God for the astounding responsibility of parenting
Jesus, Joseph had a servant heart that was shaped by his readiness
to find his place in the kingdom of God and surrender what seemed
like his natural rights in the kingdom of self. Joseph's lifelong yes
to God reveals a will shaped by Love.

Soft but Not Weak

Fortunately, living with consent—that is, living with a will that is
shaped by God's loving will, not simply by discipline and determination—is not limited to the first century or the Holy Family.
Chances are good that your life has been touched by someone like
this. Mine has. Let me illustrate what such people are like by telling
you about my friend and former pastor, Rev. Robert Harvey.

Bob was a gentle man whose being oozed with integrity, gentleness and strength. His love for people in general translated into
a deep personal caring for whoever he encountered, this being
readily apparent in the undivided attention and availability he rou-
tinely offered others. Even a relatively casual encounter with him
was enough to let you know that he was somebody special. After I

gave the eulogy at his funeral, a number of people who lived in his neighborhood but had never been in his home or church told me of ways this remarkable man had touched them. And those of us who were fortunate enough to be in even closer to the heartbeat of that life had been blessed even more richly.

Real gentleness comes from restrained strength. This was true of my friend. He had obvious strength of will and strength of character. He was not someone who could be easily manipulated. But he could be easily bent. This was because he was soft, not brittle. He was humble and he was tender. He was also deeply compassionate. His will was in the service of the love that was pervasive in his character—love not of himself but of God and of others.

There is nothing to fear in strength when the will is subservient to love. At the most vulnerable and broken point in my life, when I found my professional and personal life imploding, I found it easy to share my overwhelming sense of failure and the depths of my self-doubt with Bob. There was absolute safety in the space he gave me. It was a safety that came from total confidence in the fact of his love for me. His will pointed him toward God, and that is what made him both safe and available for me and the many others who were nurtured by his willing life of consent. His heart was God's heart, and the Love-shaped willingness that he offered made him soft but not weak.

What I am describing is more a matter of heart than of personality. You may have been blessed to know someone who showed the same gentle strength but whose personality was quite different from my friend's. But you know when you are in the presence of someone who has learned to surrender his or her will to perfect love.

❧

Take a few moments for prayerful reflection on how much your own willing is motivated by love and how much by obligation.

What would change for you if you were to live with the sort of submissive openness to God's will that we saw in Joseph? How would your choosing and acting be different if it were all motivated by love—love of God, love of others and love of God's world? What might God be inviting you to do differently if you hear an invitation to allow your will to be softened by love?

Only love is strong enough to transform willfulness. And only God's love is up to the job of leading us into the freedom of willing surrender to God's will. Living this life of consent is not the result of determination and discipline. It comes from learning to choose God, moment by moment, day by day.

living in Gods love would allow me to spread his message out of pure excitement to show others the truth rather than obligation.

four

Choosing God

As a serious young Christian (much too serious, I think in retrospect!), I used to think about God's will a lot. That topic got a great deal of emphasis in the rather earnest and humorless Christian tradition in which I was raised. But for all this emphasis and all my seriousness, I seriously missed the point of God's will. I incorrectly assumed that it primarily applied to behavior—most specifically to choices of vocation, marriage, and sin versus righteousness. So if a person had already settled into a job, chosen a husband or wife, or wasn't facing an obvious decision whether or not to sin, God's will receded into the background.

What a shamefully small view of God's love! Can God's dreams for us really be limited to a few moments in life—isolated decisions and major transition points? Is God really irrelevant to our experience of daily existence, to the rhythms of our daily life? I no longer think so. I no longer believe that God is simply interested in your job, your decision about whom (or whether) to marry or your success in sin avoidance. As incredible as it sounds, God is interested in *you!* God longs for your friendship, not simply your compliance.

gods word + gods spirit = gods will

WILL AND PRESENCE

In spite of how we sometimes think of it, God's will is not imper-sonal—reducible to a code of law. Nor is it primarily about what we do. It is deeply personal and inherently relational. And it can never be meaningfully separated from God's Spirit and presence.

Some Christians think of God's will strictly in terms of the Bible. But while the Bible is God's Word, it cannot be properly interpreted without God's Spirit. God's will cannot be known apart from the presence and activity of God's Spirit. Divine will is therefore indispensably connected to divine presence. If God is not present in the Person of the Holy Spirit, God remains absent to us no matter how many Bibles we have accumulated around us.

But what has this to do with choosing God's will over mine? I am convinced that one of the most precious gifts God wants to give us is an abiding sense of divine presence. This is why Jesus sent his Spirit when he left Earth to return to the Father—so that we would not be left alone as orphans (John 14:16-18). God longs to banish our loneliness and sense of autonomous existence with the gift of divine presence. Learning to will God's way begins with learning to attend to God's presence.

I am writing these words at 3:00 a.m. Frequent travel between Canada and Southeast Asia has left me with chronic sleep distur-bance that never quite clears up before the next trip. But I awoke this morning after a couple of hours of sleep with a sense of blessing and anticipation. Having fallen asleep after a brief prayer review of my experience of God yesterday, I awoke with an immediate sense—or at least an expectation—of God's presence. Even before I glanced at the clock, the darkness of the room and quietness of the streets told me this was another middle-of-the-night awak-ening. Often my first reaction to this is irritation, quickly followed by concern about how I will manage the demands of the upcoming day with sleep deprivation. But today my first thought was the words of a favorite verse of Scripture.

> I say this prayer to you, Yahweh,
>   for at daybreak you listen for my voice;
> and at dawn I hold myself in readiness for you,
>   I watch for you. (Psalm 5:3)

Knowing that God is eagerly waiting for my awareness to divine presence is a great help in my own spiritual attentiveness. I watch for the One who is already watching for me. I seek to attend to the One who is constantly attending to me. Is it any wonder that I awoke this morning with a sense of blessedness? Oh that this would be my first awareness every day. For day by day God's presence is constant and my blessedness unfalteringly abundant.

Turning our will toward God begins with turning our attention. There can be no relationship without attention.

ATTENDING TO PRESENCE

It is possible to know God's presence throughout the day, not just in the first moments after waking. And we can know this presence not just when doing religious or spiritual things but in the regular activities of regular days. This is the testimony of many Christians who have learned to cultivate an ongoing awareness of divine presence.

Brother Lawrence, the humble seventeenth-century monk who spent his day attempting to commune with God as he washed dishes in the monastery kitchen, describes the results of this discipline in his book *The Practice of the Presence of God*.[1] With profound humility—telling his story in the third person as the experience of "one of the brothers"—he reported that after more than forty years of seeking nothing more than an awareness of God's presence, this had become his almost constant experience. His life had become his prayer, and his prayer his life. Any distinction between the two was meaningless as he spent his day with God—sometimes in the worded communication of spontaneous interchanges but often simply in the comfortable communion of two who had spent enough time together to make words unnecessary.

Brother Lawrence's spiritual discipline was really remarkably simple: he described it as a loving turning of his eyes toward God at all times. His prayer method is in fact a discipline for the cultivation of a love relationship. How does one come to love another but by paying loving attention to that person? Love inclined his attention—and his will—toward God. Love, not discipline, was the motive for his habit of turning his attention toward God. His love-shaped choosing of God's presence and God's will came to be his vocation and deepest fulfillment.

Brother Lawrence's testimony speaks powerfully to me. I find myself taking his slim little book off the shelf and rereading it whenever I need encouragement in the process of the transformation of my willing.

His is not the only testimony of the possibility of the transformation of our willing through the transformation of our consciousness. Frank Laubach presents a modern-day sequel to Brother Lawrence's testimony by describing a practice that began when he sought to turn his attention toward God for one second out of every minute of every waking hour of the day. Soon this increased to a majority of most minutes of most hours. After only four weeks he reported the following: "I feel simply carried along each hour, doing my part in a plan which is far beyond myself. This sense of cooperation with God in little things is what so astonishes me, for I never have felt this way before. . . . I must work, to be sure, but there is God working along with me." [2]

Others, who are known to me personally but are too humble to let me tell their story for fear it might identify them, have come to know the same blessing of a life filled with God-consciousness.

None claims that every minute of every day involves thoughts of God. But all attest that as in the experience of Brother Lawrence and Frank Laubach, when they notice that some time has passed without awareness of God, there is an almost immediate pull of their attention back toward God and a surge of joy associated with fresh awareness of God's presence. *aka baptism*

Choosing God is not supposed to be a one-time experience. It should be the minute-by-minute act of willing God's will by attending to divine presence. For how could one be in the presence of one's lover and not seek to do and be whatever would bring joy to the lover? God's presence draws us into God's loving will. If we allow ourselves to be aware of divine presence, it will change our willing. But it does require turning our attention toward God.

PRESENCE IN THE WORD → *"a living thing"*

One of the places where we should expect to most dependably encounter God's presence is the Bible. By its own testimony, the Word of God is a living thing (Hebrews 4:12). It is the breath of the living God. How tragic that we often treat it merely as a text to be studied or a compilation of dogmas to be believed and defended.

Like many other modern Christians, I have found that the ancient Christian practice of *lectio divina* has done wonders to vitalize my engagement with Scripture. Literally meaning "divine reading," *lectio divina* is designed to allow the Word of God to penetrate our heart and lead us into an intimate relationship with the Lord. It involves reading (or listening to) a short passage and expectantly waiting for the word or phrase that is God's personal word for today. It takes seriously the truth that the Word of God is always alive and active, always fresh and new.

The mechanics of *lectio* are less important than the desire that should be behind it. The Lord who promises that if you seek you will find is the Lord who waits for you within the Word. Approach it, therefore, with expectancy. Anticipate an encounter and a gift—a word or phrase that will be God's personal word for you today.

Reading a short passage with my heart and spirit open—not trying to find something or make something happen but simply waiting for the gift that the Spirit of God has for me today—has brought the Bible back to life for me. Learning to expect that my daily morsel of Scripture will contain spiritual manna that will nourish my soul and meet my present spiritual needs has helped me discern the presence of God in the Word of God.

Although *lectio divina* is not the only way I read Scripture, it has become the primary one. It has made the Bible fresh and personal once again and has helped me meet God in a way that is immediate and vital. It has brought me back into contact with the Word behind the words.

Neither God's will nor God's Word can be reduced to the words of the Bible—something that can be kept automatically available as it sits on a bookcase or night table. "God's Word is always a happening—an event which creates faith and sets people free for hope. . . . The human words of the Bible are the occasion and possibility of God's speaking to us."[3] How different our encounter with Scripture would be if we really believed this, if we really knew from experience that this was true!

WILL AND AWARENESS

God is present in Scripture. But divine presence is far from restricted to the Bible. I used to pray that God would be present with me. I no longer do so. Now my prayer is that *I might know* God's presence with me.

Richard Rohr reminds us, "We cannot attain the presence of God. We're already totally in the presence of God. What's absent is awareness."[4] Willing God's will begins with lifting our spiritual eyes heavenward. Prayer follows awareness. In fact, it springs forth automatically. But we shouldn't start talking until we are aware of Presence. After all, it's rude to barge into anyone's presence already talking!

Ultimately, awareness holds much more transformative power than will. Simone Weil discovered this in her remarkable but brief thirty-four years of life, and her writings give one of the clearest discussions of the dynamic relationship of will and awareness that we possess. She points out the enormous limitations of trying to change ourselves by resolution of the will. She argues that doing so enhances only self-control and the tightness of the soul that we call pride. Change that results from attention, on the other hand, is dramatically different.

Attention for Weil is not the active mental process of concentration that is involved in what people usually refer to as "paying attention." Rather, it is suspending our thoughts and allowing awareness to develop. It is therefore more like prayerful openness than like thinking. In fact, she argues, "attention, taken to its highest degree, is the same thing as prayer. It presupposes faith and love. Absolutely unmixed attention is prayer."[5] (Weil's ideas are psychologically and spiritually profound—and quite complex. Don't allow yourself to be bogged down by this and the next paragraph if these thoughts seem overly technical or obtuse.)

Will, she argues, is the wrong way of seeking. When we "will" something, our focus is fixed on the problem or desired outcome. Attention, on the other hand, is bound up with desire and always involves awareness of "the distance . . . between what we are and what we love."[6] Transformation happens, she argues, when we desire something, not when we simply try to accomplish or obtain it. Every effort in the direction of change that comes simply from the exercise of the will is costly to the soul. Change that results from attention and desire demands the passivity of our natural powers. She writes: "I have to deprive all that I call 'I' of the light of my attention and turn it on to that which cannot be conceived. . . . [It must be] turned with love towards God."[7]

What Weil is saying is that the things we can obtain by virtue of mere willpower are trivial when contrasted to the things we can receive when longing and attention are directed toward God. We cannot, for example, will the presence of God. We can only allow love to draw us into it. Nor can we will the important changes that we know in the depths of our soul to be required for our wholeness. We can only *allow* them to be the fruit of living life in the awareness of the presence of Perfect Love.

Rabbi Shapiro tells how one day a young Hasidic Jew approached Reb Yerachmiel ben Yisrael. "Rebbe," the young man asked with seriousness, "what is the way to God?" The rebbe looked up from his work and answered: "There is no way to God, for God is not other than here and now. The truth you seek is not hidden from you; you are hiding from it."[8]

This is the truth that has been proclaimed by all the great Christian mystics across Christian history. And it is the truth taught from cover to cover of the Bible. In his Areopagus sermon Paul declares that God "is not far from any of us, since it is in him that we live, and move, and exist" (Acts 17:28). God is closer than our next breath. In fact, Job reminds us that not only is God the source of each breath, but each breath is God's breath (Job 27:3). How much more intimate could our relationship with God be? God is not absent. It is we who fail to notice divine presence. It's all a matter of awareness.

RECEPTIVE OPENNESS

Choosing God begins with receptive openness and attentiveness to God. Although God occasionally crashes through our walls of indifference, normally if we are to discern divine presence we must be spiritually attentive. But choosing God involves more than attentiveness. It also involves receptivity and openness to engagement and response.

God is not properly pursued as an object of curiosity. Openness to God must be an openness not simply to ideas or information but to personal encounter. God is not an object to be examined under a microscope like a piece of rock. God is a Person—in fact, the prototype of personhood. And persons can be engaged only with personal openness and encounter.

Gordon Smith asks: "Are we open to the Lord, to the depths of our being? Is there first and foremost an abandonment of our selves, our whole selves, to the love and goodness of God?"[9] Apart from such openness we are not truly seeking God, even though we may be seeking something *from* God. If, on the other hand, we are open to God and seeking to be attentive to divine presence, we will know that presence. For as we are seeking and attentive to God, we can be sure that God is seeking and attentive to us.

Gray Temple is someone who is open to God. In his book *When God Happens* he tells his story as a self-described "ultra-liberal-pacifist-theological-existentialist" Episcopal priest who was busy serving God but never really expected a relationship with God that could be called personal. In fact, such language was embarrassing and distasteful to him. After an extended series of God-encounters, he still describes himself as an ultra-liberal-pacifist-theological-existentialist, with one important difference—he now actively loves Jesus. All that God asked for in this process was consent. The initiative in the establishment of a love relationship was all on the part of God.

Noting the preconditions to knowing God's presence and initiative in establishing a love relationship, Canon Temple suggests that it begins with nothing more complicated than a desire to encounter God—for God's own sake, not simply to receive some specific fruit or divine favor. He offers a personal example.

I'm typing this paragraph in the Atlanta airport before dawn, one of fifty-five stand-by passengers on a heavily over-sold flight. I'm praying that God will slip me past the others—the others who are glowering at my clerical garb with the superstitious suspicion that I possess unfair supernatural pull. . . . As I sit here wanting that seat, praying for it, resenting my rivals, the presence of God is difficult to feel. But as I step back from my specific desire and ask simply to be aware of God's presence in this airport, the whole atmosphere on this concourse changes. The people seem more attractive, surprisingly "dear," though that's a word that doesn't often occur to me. I wouldn't trade this moment for a business-class seat to Paris.[10]

Fr. Louis Evely is also a man who has lived a life open to God, a life that has been full—therefore—of the same sort of God-invasions. Noting that God's very character is revelation, he suggests that God must self-express.

> Since He's Love, He must give Himself, share His secrets, communicate with us, and reveal Himself to anyone who wants to listen. His sole delight is to confide in us and give Himself to us. . . . From the very start it was man who walked away, man who turned a deaf ear to God's words. . . . But God's never wearied of talking to us. He keeps reopening the conversation, hoping we'll listen; He keeps offering His friendship, however often we spurn Him.[11]

God does not fail to offer presence to those who are attentive and open. No one can put him- or herself at God's disposal without, as Evely puts it, "being acted upon, cured and consoled, moved and snatched up."[12]

WHEN GOD SEEMS ABSENT

I winced as I quoted that last sentence. I think of a number of people I know who are open to God and seeking to be attentive to divine presence but who feel that God has been tremendously slow in showing up for the rendezvous. We must therefore pause for a moment to consider this troubling experience, which is familiar to all of us if we dare to be honest.

There are at least three reasons God can be present with us—as close, in fact, as our next breath—yet seem absent: God's hiddenness, the limitations of the senses and objectivity as ways of knowing God, and our failure to understand God's language of self-revelation.

The experience of the absence of God is a poignant reminder of what should be, but often is not, obvious. God is not like us. We are like God in some important ways, but God is so much more, so much other, so much beyond, that we miss the divine when we seek a god made in our likeness. We miss the divine when we fail to recognize that the Christian God of self-revelation is also often a hidden God.

The kind of god I would likely create could be produced at my beck and call, turned off and on like water in a tap. But the Christian God surprisingly often seems hidden or removed and is beyond our manipulation and control. This frustrating independence of God is, according to John of the Cross, one of the best proofs that God is not the product of our imagination. God can be known only in faith and in love.

Because objective ways of knowing serve us well in many spheres of life, we are sometimes troubled by the limitations of objective knowing in the encounter with God. I know it is sunny and warm outside today because when I go to the window or step out the door I feel the warmth and I can see the sun. But God—who is Spirit—cannot be known by these objective sensory means. The author of *The Cloud of Unknowing* describes the darkness (or unknowing) that must always exist between humans and God as the result of the limitation of sensory and rational knowing of the divine. God cannot be known by thought, he says: "It is love alone that can reach God in this life, and not knowing."[13] Reaching out to God with longing that is willing to be turned into love is a form of knowing. And it leads to a knowing that is infinitely deeper and more personal than objective knowing. It leads to subjective knowing in faith.

Not only does God sometimes seem to withdraw as a means to deepen our faith, not only is God hidden from the scrutiny of our senses and rationality, but at times when the divine seems absent it is because we are looking in the wrong places. We think we have never seen Jesus? Remember his words: "I was hungry and you gave me food; I was thirsty and you gave me drink; I was a stranger and you made me welcome" (Matthew 25:35). The Christian God has an inscrutable habit of turning up where we least expect to find the divine—in the hungry, the poor and the oppressed.

Jesus promised to be with us always, even to the end of time (Matthew 28:20), and he can be counted on to keep his word. When we fail to sense his presence, it is because we have not properly attuned our attention to the God who is, in truth, present: "Only when we give up fashioning Him in our image and seeking Him where we think He should be—only then will we perceive Him.... Only when we love Him enough to prefer his ways to ours, His language and His will—only then will we discover Him."[14]

It is possible to learn God's language. But the divine language is a language of presence more than of words. Although the One who created words can and certainly does use them to communicate, God's primary communication medium is the Word already shared with us. God speaks through Jesus (the Word made flesh), Scriptures (the Word of God), creation (the fruit of the Word) and the Holy Spirit (the Spirit of the Word). God promised to be with us every day until the end of time. Learning to attend to this presence is therefore learning God's preferred language. This is an essential part of choosing God.

Choosing God's Way

It is important to recognize, however, that our choice to surrender to the kingdom of God cannot arise out of the kingdom of self. Anything we do within the kingdom of self is done by means of willpower, and that is not enough to enter or live within the kingdom of God. Rather, we must allow God's action in us—God's Spirit—to be the agent and dynamic of our choosing. What God desires is our consent, not our willpower.

So often we seem to get this wrong. Tragically, it is often those who are most earnest in their Christ-following that most rely on their own will to do so. Often it is those who place the most emphasis on surrender to God that have the most trouble doing so. Why? As they sing "I surrender all," and as they hear the preacher again ask if they are ready to "place their all on the altar," they respond to the rising waves of inner guilt with resolution, not surrender. With clenched teeth and steeled determination they promise themselves, *This time I am going to do this once and for all! This time I really mean business! This time I'm finally ready to surrender.* But surrender that is fueled by willpower is no more genuine than surrender that is fueled by guilt.

Willing in a willful manner (that is, relying on willpower) is still living a willful life. The kingdom of self and the kingdom of God are like oil and water; they just do not mix. Genuine surrender does not depend on discipline and resolution. It is leaving all that behind and being seduced by Love, even if that takes time. Seductions always do!

Choosing God is becoming aware of God by an act of attention or thought and then letting go. It is inviting God into your moment and then turning that moment over to God. It is openness to divine presence and consent to God's reign in your life. It is praying with longing that God's kingdom will come and that God's reign of love will be actualized in you and in the whole world. It is allowing God's desire to become yours, God's Spirit yours. It is opening your clenched fists of dogged determination and giving up. This is why it is called *surrender*.

The concept of choosing God is trivialized when we reduce it to the point of first making a conscious decision for Christ. This is necessary but not sufficient. To fail to recognize the difference is to confuse the first step on the journey with the whole journey.

Another way the notion of choosing God is trivialized is to reduce surrender to matters of morality. Thinking about God and affirming divine will is a powerfully helpful means of resisting temptation. But again, this is not the only time we should be choosing God. To do so is to use God for sin avoidance rather than receive the gift of divine presence. It is God's love and friendship that we need, not simply techniques for accomplishing God's will.

God wants to take up residence in every atom of our being, every moment of our existence. God wants to be present in the deep places of both our daytime consciousness and our nighttime unconsciousness. God wants to finish the work of transformation begun at our conversion. But we must give our assent. We must be open to receiving the trust that God will give us so that our life may be a *yes* to the initiatives of divine love.

God wants our attentiveness to the divine to be so habitual that we go through our days—figuratively, definitely not literally!—with our palms upturned, hands open and gaze heavenward. In every circumstance of our life our question should be *Where is God in this?* With every breath we are invited to make an offering of gratitude for and remembrance of our blessings. In every encounter, with stranger or intimate, we are given a chance to see the divine reflection. In every moment we are offered an opportunity for our longing for God's kingdom to be the framework within which we choose and act.

Take a few moments to reflect on your own choosing of God, not simply your choosing of God's will. How would tomorrow be different if you awoke with an awareness that God had preceded you into that day and was listening for your voice, watching for your appearance (Psalm 5:3)? How would your reading or hearing of Scripture be different if it contained an eager expectation of personal encounter?

Dare to encounter the courtship of the Divine Lover of your soul! Dare to allow God to draw you toward surrender, not out of obligation but out of desire. Invite the Spirit of God to so capture your heart that your willing will follow. We cannot simply will surrender to God's kingdom. But we can allow God's love to draw us toward a surrender that is not the result of our willing but the culmination of our desires.

five

Will and Desire

I recently had an interesting conversation with a friend who just finished reading the first book in this trilogy, *Surrender to Love*. He didn't like it. He told me the title had put him off because it suggested a spirituality of passivity and weakness. Having broken through his procrastination and finally gotten down to reading it, he said his initial judgment was only more strongly reinforced.

My friend is a strong character whose life and spirituality is characterized by action, commitment and idealism. He despises anything that smacks of resignation or abnegation of personal power and responsibility. His work is his prayer, and he takes up what he understands to be God's work in the world with zeal, faithfulness and passion that put me to shame. I too easily settle for ideas. My friend cannot rest until ideas are translated into action that makes a difference for Lifeboat Earth and those of us who inhabit it. The very concept of surrender was anathema to him. Clearly he would never have read the book if I had not inconveniently given him a copy.

After we discussed the concept of surrender for a while, my friend asked what I was presently writing. I shuddered to tell him. I could just anticipate his reaction to the idea of choosing God's will over ours. But seeing no easy way to avoid the question, I gave him the executive summary of the book. His response shocked me: "Choosing God's will over ours makes good sense to me," he said. "Anybody who has ever tried to change anything significant about themselves has to know how useless the human will really is. We are not losing much by giving it up."

I was completely taken by surprise. I had assumed my friend lived by the strength of his will. But as we talked more about it, I came to see that he was right when he said his passions directed his life much more than his will. He drew his energy from the causes to which he was fervently committed. His will was in the service of the basic allegiances and directions of his heart—the things in which he most passionately believed and to which his life was devoted. His will, he said, could help keep him on track with things he already deeply valued but was quite useless for getting him things he merely wanted.

My friend's comments lead us to what I want to explore in this chapter—the relationship between will and desire. His understanding of the nature of human willing contains some important insights that will, we shall see, lead us to a better understanding of what it means to choose God's will.

CHOOSING WITH THE HEART

In the previous chapters we have seen some of the limitations of the will. Naked willpower tends to produce pride and rigidity. Unchecked by love, it tends to make us mechanical and moralistic, impoverishing the soul and sapping our vitality. As a form of seeking, will keeps us focused on our self. While it is, of course, essential in directing our effort and unquestionably helpful in accomplishing important things, on its own it is seriously limited as an agent of transformation. More important, on its own it is not up to the task of aligning us with the will of God.

But resolve and determination are not the only way to choose. We can also allow our will to be led by our heart. The Hebrew psalmists knew about heart-choosing of God and have much to teach us about the role of desire in willing. Read and savor a small sample of the ways they express their longing for God.

God, you are my God, I am seeking you,
my soul is thirsting for you,
my flesh is longing for you. . . .
On my bed I think of you,
I meditate on you all night long. . . .
I sing for joy in the shadow of your wings;
my soul clings close to you. (Psalm 63:1, 6-7)

As a doe longs
    for running streams,
so longs my soul
    for you, my God.
My soul thirsts for God,
    the God of life. (Psalm 42:1-2)

Like thirsty ground, I yearn for you. (Psalm 143:6)

One thing I ask of Yahweh,
    one thing I seek:
to live in the house of Yahweh
    all the days of my life,
to enjoy the sweetness of Yahweh
    and to consult him in his Temple. (Psalm 27:4)

How my soul yearns and pines
    for Yahweh's courts!
My heart and my flesh sing for you
    to the living God. (Psalm 84:2)

To Yahweh you say, "My Lord,
you are my fortune, nothing else but you."...
So my heart exults, my very soul rejoices,
my body, too. (Psalm 16:2, 9)

Here is no teeth-clenching willful determination to follow God.
Here we find no hint of a resolve based on willpower. What we
have is people who are following their heart—a heart captured by
God's heart. Determination followed devotion. In contrast to a
choosing that is led by will, their focus was on the object of their
love, not themselves.

God does not want obedience as the fruit of our willful determination. God wants surrender as the choice of the heart. For what
we long for in our heart we will pursue with the totality of our
being—not simply with the resolve of our will.

THE HEART'S DESIRES

The human journey—particularly our spiritual journey—is shaped
by our deepest desires. More often than we expect, we get what
we most desire. This is why it is crucial that our basic heart direction be solidly grounded in God and that we allow God to
purify our desires.

My desire for respect has had a powerful—although not always
good—influence on my journey. I have often gotten what I desired,
but looking back I wish I had desired respect less and intimacy
more. Respect has too often kept others at a safe distance and kept
me content with an offering of admiration. Intimacy—both with
God and with others—would have been, and is becoming, much
more deeply satisfying as it draws me into relationships of love and
interdependence.

No matter how they appear, desires are deeply spiritual. When
understood superficially they appear to often point to our self and

our personal gratification. But as Margaret Silf reminds us, our deepest desires prove that the universe is not centered on ourselves, because they require that we reach out and move on. Deepest desires are always fulfilled "not in our arriving but in our journeying; not in the finding but in the searching."[1] For truly it is in the searching that we are found.

Despite what you may have heard, Christian spirituality is not about the crucifixion of desire. Rather it is about the distillation and focusing of desire. It is about discovering the freedom of desiring nothing more than God and then enjoying with detachment every other blessing and gift.

Ultimately, the human will is incapable of choosing God's will over ours unless it operates in partnership with desire. Without desire—distilled and purified by surrender to God's loving will—our willing produces rigidity rather than vitality. When we rely on the will alone, we become machinelike. If we are ruled by our passions alone, we become animal-like. We become fully human only when will and desire are in balance and when both are transformed by Perfect Love. Once we have drunk deeply of that love, nothing else will satisfy our heart. Our seeking of God will come from a Love-shaped place deep within us. Our fundamental longing will be a thirst for Living Water.

A moment ago I suggested that we must be careful what we desire because we may get it. But desires are even more important than this. The truth is that our desires influence more than our acquisitions. They also shape our being. Thomas Merton puts it this way: "Life is shaped by the end you live for. You are made in the image of what you desire."[2]

A desire for wealth leads to greed, envy and dissatisfaction. A desire for power saps compassion, just as a desire for reputation feeds self-preoccupation. And a desire for respect—as I know too well—leads to an overinvestment in image.

Every idolatrous desire—that is, everything that we love and desire more than God—tends ultimately to diminish our humanity and damage our soul.

In contrast, a desire for God leads to fulfillment of that longing and enhancement of our being. Hunger for God will not go unanswered, because it is a gift from God. Our longing is already an answer from our heart as it is stirred by God's Spirit. No one who seeks God fails to find God, because she or he is already found by God. In seeking we are found. In longing we express God's desire, God's longing evoking our own.

A wonderful description of this interaction of the longings of the soul and those of God comes from the thirteenth century Mechthild of Magdeburg.

The soul speaks:

"God, you are my lover,
My longing,
My flowing stream,
My sun,
And I am your reflection."

God answers:

"It is my nature that makes me love you often,
For I am love itself.
It is my longing that makes me love you intensely,
For I yearn to be loved from the heart.
It is my eternity that makes me love you long,
For I have no end."[3]

We may be tempted to feel that the desiring of God is all on our end. But our desiring originates in God's desiring of us. As Janet Ruffing states: "Our desires, our wants, our longings, our outward and inward searching—when uncovered, expressed, and recognized—all lead to the Divine Beloved.... All our desires ultimately lead us to God."[4]

The journey of desire may lead us to byways and cul-de-sacs, but if we follow it we will ultimately be led to the Divine Beloved. We may not know what it is we long for, but our deepest longings are God-given because they always point toward the divine.

KNOWING OUR DESIRES

But can this be true? Can it really be that the things I most deeply want point me toward God? Can it be that these same things tell me something about what God most deeply wants for me? Can it be true that my desires reflect in some important ways God's own desires?

I suspect there are a number of reasons we doubt this. First, most of us have been conditioned to expect that we will never get the things we most deeply want. Our deepest desires and longings seem to be therefore simply set-ups for frustration. They are dangerous. Consequently, they remain unexamined and unknown. They may unconsciously point us toward God, but if they do, we would not be any more aware of that fact than of their essential nature.

Beyond this, most of us harbor a deep-seated suspicion that God's desires for us and ours for ourselves share no common ground. We suspect that if our desires are to be fulfilled, it will be at the expense of God's—fulfillment that will have to be stolen from God. Christian spirituality, we mistakenly believe, has to do with the crucifixion of our desires, even of desire itself.

As a result, most of us do not know our deepest desires. We may know our superficial wants ("I want a new car" or "I want a holiday") but not our deeper longings. Unfortunately, the superficial wants and desires we can most easily identify are often those that are most disordered and most in need of purification. This only reinforces our sense that our desires are at best irrelevant to the spiritual journey and at worst seriously in opposition to it.

The only way to know our deepest desires is to start with the surface desires that we can access and to follow them downward to their underlying longings. This, as we shall see, then allows us to identify those desires that are most in need of refining.

Calla illustrates this process. When I first met her, Calla's longings were all focused on her desire to be married and have children. Lacking a significant relationship with a man and deeply aware of the relentless ticking of her biological clock, she felt her dreams slipping through her fingers. She was bitter and miserable.

Calla seemed puzzled when I asked her about her deepest longings. She felt she had told me everything that was to be told when she said she wanted to be married and have a child. But as we explored this further, Calla was able to see that beneath what she had thought of as ultimate desires was something more basic— a longing to feel needed and loved. It was also not hard to discern a longing to feel connected to others and to life itself. Marriage and mothering held for her the hope of meeting these basic needs. But her longing was not truly for a man or a baby. It was for love and significance. This was a longing that pointed toward God. It arose from the God-shaped empty space within her that matched the Calla-shaped inner space within God—longing answering longing. But until she saw the ultimate nature of her desires, she remained idolatrously locked onto marriage and motherhood as the only potential source of her fulfillment.

These core needs, like all core needs, are spiritual—not because love is somehow especially spiritual but because it is a need that ultimately can be met only in God. Our need for love points us toward God. So do our other core needs—needs for safety and security, identity, significance, self-expression and fulfillment.

Created as an expression of God's desire, our essential being reflects and is shaped by divine desire. Our life is a response to this fundamental source of our being. Our heart responds to it imperfectly, because our heart allegiances remain divided. But the heartbeat of God's desire can still be discerned within the pulse of our deepest desires. For our desires are truly always derivatives—distorted as they may be—of God's desires.

Our deepest desires contain residual traces of God's desires for us and always therefore point toward God. Thus deep longings are always spiritual. But our response to them is not always life-giving. Jesus tells us that where our treasure is, there our hearts will also be (Matthew 6:21). Too often we seem unable to be content with the treasure of God's person, seeking additional things we feel will add to our happiness—treasures of image, possession and accomplishment. Our desires become distorted and disordered. When this happens, they no longer reliably lead us toward God. Instead they lead us into frustration and despair, for nothing in this world can ever satisfy the deepest heart longings that were intended to point us toward God.

Purifying Our Desires

If we are honest, we all know something about disordered desires. Most of us know the possibility of forming a false attachment to someone, looking to them to meet needs that can never be met by any human. Or if we have never felt the fleeting gratification of such an idolatrous attachment, perhaps we—like Calla—know the desire for it. Most of us also realize that we can form the same sort of false attachment to possessions, money being perhaps the easiest object for this. Many of us also know disordered desire that comes from a false attachment to reputation and image.

One of the ways I have found helpful to distinguish between ordered and disordered desires is the particular, though sometimes subtle, effect each has on me. Ordered—or purified—desires expand me and connect me to others and the world in life-enhancing ways.

Disordered desires suck me into myself and rather than adding vitality to life, leach it away. This is because ordered desires spring from willingness and surrender, while disordered ones are my willful attempt to arrange for my own happiness and fulfillment.

When I desire nothing more than God alone, I experience a deep sense of well-being and connectedness. Paradoxically, this is a longing that leaves me feeling not empty but complete. It is a longing that draws me not only toward God but also toward others. It is a longing that leaves me feeling open and alive.

In contrast, when my lust for respect rears its ugly head, I become aware of a feeling of deficit. There is something that I think I need in order to feel complete, and this something is outside of me, beyond me. Thinking I can produce it by my own efforts rather than receive it as a gift, I willfully set out to get it by sacrificing reality on the altar of appearances and hoping that others will notice the appearance. But because this involves treating people as objects—potential sources of the soothing balm of admiration to which I am addicted—I feel cut off from those whose esteem I seek. And because the choice of appearance over reality always involves turning my back on God, I feel equally cut off from life and vitality.

But why talk about this as a disordered desire? Why not simply call it sin?

While it *is* sinful—as is anything that springs from the kingdom of self, any idolatrous attempt to live independently of surrender to God—I find it helpful to think of it as a disordered desire because this language reminds me that at its core it is something good. At the core of my desire to be viewed with respect is a deeper God-given desire for love. The love that I really desire and most deeply need is not, however, dependent on my performance. The love I most deeply long for is the only love that can truly set me free—the perfect and absolutely unconditional love of God.

How, then, should we deal with disordered desires? What can we do to purify these distortions of God-given longings?

We cannot purify our own desires. So don't fall into the trap of taking this on as a spiritual self-improvement project. Instead, lift yourself to God in the midst of your disordered state and allow God to undertake the necessary transformation.

Only prayer can order a disordered inner life. While this may seem overly simplistic and possibly overly spiritual, it is absolutely true.

Prayer sorts out our desires. Notice that I did not say that in prayer *we are able* to sort out our desires. No. The sorting work is God's, not ours. Our job is to sit in God's presence and allow God to purify our desires. If this does not seem practical enough, you have not spent enough time sitting in silence in God's presence. Words may be coming between you and God.

Silence in the presence of God belongs to the core of prayer. It deepens our awareness of both ourselves and God. For it is in the stillness of silent prayer that we learn what our own desires most truly are. It is here that God reveals us to ourselves. "Examine me and know my heart, probe me and know my thoughts" (Psalm 139:23) is not, as it appears, a request that God would know me but that God would show that known self to me. And where God does this most dependably is in silent prayer where we center ourselves in God.

Prayer is the place of divine transformation because it is the place in which our hearts are slowly transformed into the heart of God. Prayer is the place where we discover that our deepest desire is nothing other than God alone. This is the purification of desire.

Only when we are willing to desire nothing more than God can we experience the freedom of truly enjoying all things. Christian spirituality does not involve the destruction of desire. Rather it involves realignment of our desires by turning our hearts toward the Source of all desire. God's desires become our desires.

When we long for nothing more than God, our deepest longings dependably point us toward God. This is fullness of life. Remember Jesus' words about this: "Is there a man among you who would hand his son a stone when he asked for bread? Or would hand him a snake when he asked for a fish? If you, then, who are evil, know how to give your children what is good, how much more will your Father in heaven give good things to those who ask him!" (Matthew 7:9-11). God longs to give us our heart's desires. But to receive them, we must allow God's heart to become ours. We must learn to desire as God desires. This is choosing life.

CHOOSING LIFE

Properly understood, choosing God is choosing life. If the two seem different for you, there is a vitally important dimension of God awaiting your discovery!

St. Irenaeus reminds us that the glory of God is human beings who are fully alive. God is the source and foundation of life. The breath of God, the Holy Spirit, sustains all that has life. And Jesus came to bring us abundant life—life that is so full that it points us back to God, the author of life. In so doing it gives God glory.

God longs for our fulfillment, not merely our compliance with the divine will. God is in the resurrection business, calling us to shake off our graveclothes and emerge from the tombs in which we live. God invites us to share the animating and generative life that is our origin and destiny.

Choosing God is a matter of choosing life over death. This was precisely the choice God gave Moses and then told him to pass on to the children of Israel:

> See, today I set before you life and prosperity, death and disaster. If you obey the commandments of Yahweh that I enjoin on you today, if you love Yahweh your God and follow

his ways, if you keep his commandments, his laws, his customs, you will live and increase, and Yahweh your God will bless you in the land which you are entering to make your own. But if your heart strays, if you refuse to listen, if you let yourself be drawn into worshiping other gods and serving them, I tell you today, you will most certainly perish; you will not live long in the land you are crossing the Jordan to enter and possess. I call heaven and earth to witness against you today: I set before you life or death, blessing or curse. Choose life, then, so that you and your descendants may live, in the love of Yahweh your God, obeying his voice, clinging to him; for in this your life consists. (Deuteronomy 30:15-20)

We face the same choice today, and every day. But choosing God can never be simply a matter of the will. We may achieve what we pursue with our will. But we cannot simply will God. We can only desire God and then willingly follow this desire. It is the deepest longings and desires of our heart that ultimately direct our spiritual journey. A journey into the heart of God will always involve desire for God, not simply a will to become Godlike.

In his book *Thoughts in Solitude,* Thomas Merton shares a prayer that expresses his deepest heart longings. His words reveal stunning levels of honesty combined with astounding faith.

My Lord God, I have no idea where I am going. I cannot see the road ahead of me. I cannot know for certain where it will end. Nor do I really know myself, and the fact that I think I am following your will does not mean that I am actually doing so. But, I believe that the desire to please you does in fact please you. And I hope I have that desire in all that I am doing. I hope that I will never do anything apart from that desire. And I know that if I do this you will lead me by the right road, though I may know nothing about it. Therefore I will trust you always though I may seem to be lost and in the shadow of death. I will not fear, for you are ever with me and you will never leave me to face my perils alone.[5]

This is the life of faith. But it is also a journey of desire and longing. This is the Christian spirituality journey.

Take some time to reflect on your own desires. As you sort through them, moving from accessible surface desires to the deeper longings that lie beneath them, submit everything you discover to God in prayer. Rather than making this an exercise of psychological analysis, make it a time of prayer. Dare to simply sit in stillness and silence in God's presence, allowing the Spirit of God to pray the deepest unworded prayers of your spirit. Then talk with God about what you learn about yourself. Ask God to reorder your desiring by aligning it with the desires of God's own heart.

Finally, reflect on whether your choosing of God is bringing you genuine life. Take the long view on this assessment. If your God-choosing is not making you fundamentally more alive and vital, you may be choosing the external trappings of the Christian religion rather than the life-giving inner essence of Christian spirituality. You may be choosing a spiritual self-improvement program of the kingdom of self, but you are not choosing the genuinely life-giving program of the kingdom of God.

Hear God's call to surrender to God's will as an invitation to a fullness of life that exceeds your wildest expectations and imaginings. The source of this call is the Source of everything that is truly alive. Settle for nothing less than this truly abundant and vital life in Christ.

Choosing the Cross

*O*ver the last several chapters we have seen that choosing God begins with receptive openness and attentiveness to the one Francis Schaeffer described as "the God who is there."[1] It is daring to trust our deepest longings, believing that all desire ultimately arises from God's desires for us. It is living with consent—offering our selves as a yes in response to God's YES to us.

But while choosing God brings life, that life comes through death. This is the paschal mystery that lies at the very heart of the Christian faith. True life comes from death to my efforts to live apart from surrender to God. Finding myself comes from losing myself. Christian life is always resurrection life—life that emerges from death. Resurrection life must *start* with death. Christian life starts as we deny our self, take up our cross and follow Jesus.

Following Jesus

Jesus was brutally clear about what the choice to follow him means.

> If anyone wants to be a follower of mine, let him renounce himself and take up his cross and follow me. For anyone who wants to save his life will lose it; but anyone who loses his life for my sake will find it. (Matthew 16:24-25)

Jesus could never be accused of overselling discipleship! Christ-following demands self-renunciation and requires that we embrace things we would never naturally choose—to pick up and carry the instrument of our suffering, which will become the instrument of crucifixion of our willful self.

But before we try to understand what Jesus is inviting us to do when he asks us to take up our cross and follow him, it may be helpful to reflect on what it meant for Jesus to take up his cross. When we think about this, the first thing that comes to mind is of course the physical cross he carried on the road to Calvary. But this external cross was merely the symbol of many inner crosses he had long before this day learned to bear in his choosing of God. Had he not first learned to take up these inner crosses, he would have been unable to choose the external one.

What, then, were some of the inner crosses that Jesus learned to bear long before his physical journey along the Via Dolorosa? Because of the private nature of inner crosses, we can never know for sure. But the Gospels do give us some clues.

Think, for example, of Jesus' relationship with the religious authorities who viewed him with suspicion and hostility and constantly sought to entrap him. Think of how hard it must have been for him to love those who persecuted him and turn his other cheek to those who abused him. He did this, but he did it because he chose to bear in love the people whom he would never have naturally written into the script of his life.

Even his own disciples often constituted a cross that had to be embraced. Think of the account of their inability to heal the man with epilepsy (Matthew 17:14-20). A sanitized Gospel that sought to make Jesus conform to the shape of a deity who was less than fully human would never have recorded his irritation at their lack of faith presented in this passage. Standing before the suffering man and the disciples who had been unable to heal him because of their lack of faith, Jesus spoke harsh and critical words: "Faithless and perverse generation! . . . How much longer must I be with you? How much longer must I put up with you? Bring him here to me." Jesus then rebuked the devil and cured the son.

I believe this gives us a glimpse of a private cross that Jesus had to learn to bear—his disappointment with the lack of faith he regularly encountered in people, even his own disciples. Recall that he wept over Jerusalem when confronted with the spiritual blindness of residents of the city (Luke 19:41). Think also of his enthusiastic response whenever he encountered genuine faith, even when it was in those outside the family of faith and the community of Israel—for example, the centurion who came to Jesus so his servant could be healed (Matthew 8:5-10) and the Syrophoenician woman who sought the healing of her daughter (Matthew 15:21-28). How hard it must have been for Jesus, who lived every moment of his life by faith, to be surrounded by people of little faith. This was surely a cross he had to learn to bear.

Living and working in the intimate company of Judas had to be another cross of immense weight for Jesus. He who knew the hearts of all whom he encountered (Matthew 12:25; John 2:25) had in his inner circle of closest friends one whom he knew would betray him. Daily Jesus had to choose to love Judas and offer him the chance to choose the kingdom of God over the kingdom of self. And daily he had to embrace the cross of discouragement that must have arisen as he saw where this relationship was heading.

Jesus undoubtedly had other crosses to bear. Only he could tell us what they were. The list might include loneliness. It may also have included a lack of sexual fulfillment. Quite possibly it included the sense of differentness. Everything that he would not naturally have chosen and that caused suffering became for Jesus a cross to be taken up as he followed his heart toward the heart of God.

The call to pick up our cross and follow Jesus is not necessarily—or even likely—a call to martyrdom. But, like Jesus, we can be quite certain that we will encounter suffering and face choices between saving and losing the life of our autonomous self. In the midst of this suffering we have the choice of walking with Christ on the Way of the Cross. It is precisely in the midst of these acts of self-denial that we face the opportunity to encounter resurrection life.

TAKING UP YOUR CROSS

So what exactly does it means to take up your cross and follow Jesus?

Some people trivialize the concept by claiming every hangnail or stubbed toe as their "cross." Remember—the cross is the instrument of our crucifixion, not merely the cause of a minor annoyance.

Others feel guilty when they recall Christ's invitation to take up their cross and follow him because they can't think of any suffering big enough to make them feel worthy of calling it a cross. Sometimes this makes them wonder if their Christ-following is too casual and if that is the reason they have not yet been called to suffer for the sake of Christ. Some even look with envy at those who suffer for Christ's sake and have the grace to take up that suffering as a cross. But this too is an unhelpful distortion of what Christ is teaching.

The Way of the Cross is not marked so much by the intensity of our suffering as by our willing choice of God's way over our way—no matter what distress we are experiencing, what hardship we are facing. God's way will always present us with choice points where we must decide between self-preservation and self-renunciation. Choosing self-renunciation is taking up our cross, because it always involves loss and will often occur within the context of suffering.

Taking up my cross is accepting whatever affliction I experience—no matter how great or small—and inviting Christ to walk alongside me as I carry it. It is meeting the suffering Savior in the midst of my suffering and allowing myself to be touched by his grace. Taking up my cross is accepting self-denial and sacrifice as a part of my daily life as I follow Christ. Walking this sacred Way of the Cross allows me, therefore, to participate in Christ's suffering. But more, it puts my suffering in perspective and gives it meaning, because at the end of the Way of the Cross is the resurrection.

When I think of the crosses in my life, I think not so much of the big crises where I felt great pain and distress as of the small daily choices of self-renunciation that lead to a loss of the life of my kingdom of self.

A colleague publicly lashed out at me this week for something I did not do. An equally public defense was impossible at the moment, so I quietly suffered the abuse and attempted to restrain my anger. After the incident I tried to approach him to clarify the misunderstanding. But he was unwilling to either talk or listen; he hurled further verbal abuses at me and then walked away.

I was confused and hurt. I couldn't understand what had upset him so much, and I was angry at the injustice of the situation. I felt like a victim, and I didn't like the feeling.

That night as I was prayerfully reviewing the day to see where I had been aware of God's presence and where I had not, I suddenly saw the incident in a wholly new light. Rather than being an incident of abuse, it was a cross. I had a choice. I could feel like a victim, or I could deny my "right" of self-defense or retaliation and walk the Way of the Cross. I could meet the suffering Savior in my small affliction. Jesus, better than anyone, knew what it was to suffer injustice and public humiliation. His presence was uniquely available to me in this experience of my cross.

I had a choice. But suddenly encountering Christ in the midst of this situation made the choice easy. I chose to take up my cross and follow Jesus.

My response to this epiphany of encountering Christ while walking through an ordinary day was to send my colleague an email the next morning, apologizing for anything I had done to offend or upset him and again offering to talk further about it if he wished. A small step of self-renunciation both led to and flowed from a resurrection moment of finding true life.

There is nothing very dramatic about this incident. I share it because it is so ordinary. But its very ordinariness is the reason it is so important. If, as Luke urges, we are to take up our cross daily (Luke 9:23), our cross must be things that we encounter regularly.

Some people take up the same cross day after day—physical or mental illness, the consequences of abuse, poverty, or unrelenting loneliness. Many others, like me, do not have to bear these major burdens but must similarly be prepared to embrace things we would never choose. Being unable to change these things, we have only two choices: to rail against them in anger or embrace them and turn to God for help in coping with them and meeting Jesus in them.

Taking up our cross requires that we accept the realities of our life that we wish were otherwise. As Richard Rohr reminds us: "God is found in the actual—not in the idealized."[2] There is no need to change the circumstances of our life, even of our heart, in order to meet God. But we must first accept reality. God is far too real to be found anywhere else.

THE FOOLISHNESS OF THE CROSS

What does embracing the crosses of your life have to do with choosing to follow Christ? Why did Jesus make this so central to choosing God, putting it first on his list of what it means to be a disciple?

The answer to these questions lies in the remarkable passage that follows Paul's discussion of his personal cross, something he called his "thorn in the flesh." He does not tell us what this cross was. But listen to him speak about his struggle with it and what he learned through it.

> About this thing, I have pleaded with the Lord three times for it to leave me, but he has said, "My grace is enough for you: my power is at its best in weakness." So I shall be very happy to make my weaknesses my special boast so that the power of Christ may stay over me, and that is why I am quite content with my weaknesses, and with insults, hardships, persecutions, and the agonies I go through for Christ's sake. For it is when I am weak that I am strong. (2 Corinthians 12:8-10)

Astoundingly, whatever Paul's private cross was, it became his gift. It came to be the thing of which he was most proud, his most cherished possession. The reason this cross became so valuable to him was that through it he learned the paschal mystery. He learned that life comes from death, strength from weakness.

This is the foolishness of the cross—not simply the physical cross on which Christ was crucified, but the crosses on which we experience crucifixion of the kingdom of self and the new abundant life of the kingdom of God. Paul could boast about his weakness, not his strength (2 Corinthians 12:5), because God had shown him that divine power is manifest in human weakness.

Our crosses—once embraced and carried in response to Christ's invitation to follow him as he followed the will of his heavenly Father—become the places where we meet the divine power that is the only possible agent of our transformation. The cross that I take up and carry in response to Jesus' invitation to follow him becomes the place not only of my death but also of my resurrection. The way of Christian spirituality is the Way of the Cross. There is no alternate route. The Christian life is filled with little deaths and little resurrections, little Good Fridays and little Easter Sundays. Each embrace of my cross is a further step into the kingdom of God, a kingdom we can reach only on the other side of the death of our own kingdoms and queendoms of self-sufficiency and self-determination.

The cross of Christ is an icon of transformation: "Hanging between heaven and earth ... [it puts] together what normally cannot be put together."[3] The cross reminds us that it is in pain and suffering that we experience our transformation—not in our efforts to improve ourselves or avoid sin. The cross reminds us that it is in weakness, suffering and death that we find life.

The cross is a place of tension. Taking up our cross—rather than avoiding, minimizing or reacting to it—places us squarely in a place of suffering. But God works out our transformation in the midst of the tension. This is the gift Jesus gives us when he invites us to take up our crosses and follow him.

Just as Jesus was crucified between the good thief and the bad thief, we are always crucified in the torture of opposites. We experience good and bad in our childhood. But Jesus' invitation is to accept the givens of our life and follow him. We experience love and betrayal in our marriages and friendships. But Jesus' invitation remains the same—to accept the givens of our life and follow him. We experience joy and suffering in our body. And Jesus' word to us remains constant—take up your cross and follow me.

THE CROSS AS MEETING POINT

Taking up our cross is not the same as simply resigning our self to things we cannot change. There is no transformation in such passive resignation. The route to Christian spiritual transformation is more active. It involves accepting those sources of suffering that we did not originally choose but that, being already ours, we are invited to accept. It means embracing the things that we instinctively want to eliminate. It demands a response that is totally counterinstinctual, 180 degrees opposite to what we naturally want to do.

What we want to do is either fight against the suffering or ignore it. What Jesus asks is something quite different. Taking up our cross is not, in the final analysis, choosing between whether to suffer or not. That choice is not ours. But we can choose to acknowledge the suffering rather than ignore it. And while holding it, we can choose to look toward God. If we do, we discover God looking toward us.

Taking up our cross is allowing suffering to be a place of meeting God. For no matter how great your suffering may be, God has suffered from it first. Only when we embrace the suffering that can never be avoided do we meet the God who, as Paul says, "is everything and . . . is in everything" (Colossians 3:11).

Joseph Campbell states that the cross is not only one historic moment on Calvary, but the mystery through all time and space of God's presence and participation in the agony of all living things.[4] It is just as the Apostle Paul claimed. It is in the midst of our suffering and weakness that Christ is most present. It is here that our vulnerability and weakness meet Christ's transformational power.

RESURRECTION LIFE

The Way of the Cross leads to the resurrection. Lent leads to Easter and finds its meaning and fulfillment in Easter. Without the resurrection, suffering and self-denial would make no sense.

The great gift of Christian spirituality can be stated in a single word—*life!* God has taken the symbol of death—the cross—and turned it into a symbol of life. For this to happen, Jesus had to accept his own cross, and God had to meet him in his death and transform death into life.

The crosses in our life that we take up as an act of following Jesus are similarly transformed into something we could never imagine. What appears to be loss becomes gain. What appears to be death becomes life. This is the mystery of our life in Christ.

❧

Take some time to reflect on what Jesus is asking you to do as he invites you to take up your cross and follow him. Consider the givens of your existence that you might wish to change if you had the ability to do so. What would be different if you were to embrace these realities—to accept them as part of your cross and to expect to meet God in the midst of them? Pray for eyes to see Christ in your recent sufferings and afflictions, small or large as they may be, and choose to accept these as opportunities to walk with Jesus on the Way of the Cross.

Rejoice every time you discover a new area of your life that you cannot change but would naturally wish you could. For in this weakness and inability you have the opportunity to fall into the hands of the living God. You will not fall as long as you cling to the illusion of self-control and mastery. But neither will you discover that you are held. Accept the good news that it is in your weakness that God's power is perfected. Allow your cross to become Christ's cross, and his yours. This too is choosing God. This too is learning to choose God's way and God's will.

seven

Developing a
Discerning Heart

*B*ooks and sermons on God's will usually focus on how to make decisions. Attentiveness to God at points of major decisions is important, and God's will is clearly relevant at these times. But it is equally important in the times when we face no noticeable decisions.

God's will is not primarily a matter of whether you take the job in Chicago or the one in Calgary, whether you marry this or that person, or whether you attend a Catholic or a Baptist church. God's will is that you become the person that from eternity you were destined to be—your true self-in-Christ. God's will is that you discover the fullness of life that is uniquely possible in surrendering to divine love and taking up your calling in the kingdom of God.

At the center of God's deepest desire for you is divine longing to complete your transformation. God's dream for you is that you become whole and holy as you find your identity and fulfillment in mystical union with the Lord God. Everything else is of secondary importance—of significance only as it facilitates or impedes this journey.

The choice between jobs or potential spouses may well have significant impact in this. But we miss the point of God's will when we fail to recognize that God's interest in what we do grows out of a much more fundamental interest in who we are. God's deepest dreams for us are grounded in passionate longing for intimacy with us.

The development of interpersonal intimacy always demands the development of a discerning heart. My relationship with my wife, Juliet, has taught me most of what I know about how to attend to the presence, needs and desires of someone I love. This is the whole point of a loving relationship. Love could never be satisfied with simple obedience—meeting minimal behavioral expectations and expressed wishes. My love for Juliet makes me attentive to not just her needs but her deepest longings, and I find special joy in being able to discern these longings and help her find their fulfillment.

We become *discerning* about whatever it is that we love. Discernment is knowing the heart of our beloved. This is how our heart is aligned with the heart of our lover and our intimacy deepened. And this is exactly how it works with God.

THE HEART'S DIRECTION

Although the mind has an important role to play in discernment, the function of the heart is even more basic. But don't allow yourself to think of the heart as simply the emotions. While, as we shall see, emotions have a crucial role in discernment, our *affections* are even more central to discernment. First and foremost, discernment is a matter of what I would call our *heart allegiances.* These constitute our fundamental life orientation.

Since you have read this far in this book, it is likely that your heart is basically directed toward God. It is likely that you want to surrender to God's loving will and find your place in kingdom service. As much as you may be tempted from time to time, you know there is no way in the world you could ever turn your back on the God who is absolutely incapable of turning away from you. Like mine, your fundamental life orientation is probably toward God.

When I am honest, I am forced to admit that I am not always true to this basic life direction. The competing loves of my life—happiness, comfort, image, accomplishments—may not be as satisfying as they were before my heart was given to God, but they do creep back in as countercurrents that complicate my floating in the river that is God. Still, there is no question that I clearly feel the flow of the river. I know I am being drawn along by the Spirit of God, and I know that my deepest longing is to offer a total yes of surrender to my Beloved. There is no way I want to turn around and swim with those ever-weakening eddies that still flow out of the kingdom of my self.

Think for a moment about your own basic life direction. Are you merely flirting with God—still holding off from a fundamental decision to align your heart and self with the kingdom of God? Or does God have your basic allegiance, even if from time to time the turbulence of crosscurrents complicates your floating? Think how different your life would be if you were singularly directed toward any one of these alternative gods. Your life would be vitally different, because your basic heart allegiance would be different.

As Jesus said, no one can serve two masters. No one can have more than one basic heart allegiance. We may be quite successful in fooling ourselves and others about the true nature of this basic allegiance. (Religious people are particularly good at this.) But the heart seeks singleness of direction. Purity of heart, Søren Kierkegaard reminds us, is to will one thing.

Emotions and Spirituality

Developing a discerning heart involves not just our basic heart allegiance; it also involves our emotions.

We are sometimes told that emotions are simply superficial aspects of experience, nothing more than distractions in the spiritual life. One should, the argument goes, place facts before feelings, letting our mind inform our heart. Others suggest that (despite a total absence of any biblical support) emotions have been more tainted by sin than either the intellect or the will. As a consequence, emotions are—we are told—untrustworthy and have no legitimate role in spiritual discernment.

The effects of this have gone far beyond misunderstanding of the role of emotions in spiritual discernment. Much more serious, it has produced a spirituality that is often dangerously dissociated from the psychological realities of our inner world. If our emotions were irrelevant to our spiritual life, and if it were true that God is more interested in relating to some parts of our being than to others, then our emotions would be left out of the entire conversion process. But, thank God, this is not true.

What is true, of course, is that the most superficial layer of our emotions *is* an unstable basis for decision making. We all know how volatile these wisps of feelings can be. But beneath this outermost layer of fleeting reactions to the external world and our present inner biochemical cocktail lie two other layers of affectivity.[1]

At our deepest core lie feelings that we will likely experience only at rare moments, if we are blessed enough to ever experience them. Sometimes called "unitive experiences," these transcendent moments involve an awareness of deep connectedness with God and everything else that exists. They may come during prayer, or they could as well emerge suddenly during a walk in a forest or while gazing into a starry sky. Gerald May describes them as the sudden feeling of being "swept up by life, caught in a suspended moment where time seems to stand still and awareness peaks, . . . becoming at once totally wide-awake and open."[2] We see our selves and the world with awesome clarity, and all our preoccupations, concerns and anxieties suddenly evaporate. We know God's presence in a way that has almost nothing to do with our intellect. And our feelings are equally remarkable—simply a profound sense of awe and well-being.

In the intermediate zone between these two layers of feelings lie emotions that anyone can learn to discern because they are present for all of us, even though we are not usually present to them. Here we find the place where moods (which are deeper and more persistent than feelings) reside. This is also the home of "gut feelings." In this place the boundary between emotions and intuition is very thin. Our "knowing" of what we feel at this level is not as simple as the knowing of our surface feelings. But unlike the knowing involved in unitive experiences, it is something that we can cultivate.

Attending to feelings at this level of our being demands what Henri Nouwen called solitude of heart.[3] This involves more than being alone. It is a receptive stillness that is learned in silence in the presence of God. Only here can we learn to discern the emotional movements of our heart that accompany any genuine encounter with God. We may come away from meeting God with thoughts, and we can be thankful for them. But our thoughts will never contain the vastness of the impact on our being that a divine encounter necessarily involves. To open ourselves to that impact, we must cultivate a discerning heart. This includes, as we shall see, learning to attend to emotional reactions in this intermediate zone.

CONSOLATION AND DESOLATION

No one has been more helpful in explaining what it means to develop a discerning heart than a man who lived five hundred years ago in a small village in northern Spain. His name was Iñigo Lopez. He is better known to us as Ignatius of Loyola, the founder of the Society of Jesus, commonly referred to as the Jesuits. Four centuries before the rise of modern psychology, Ignatius gave us the most psychologically grounded understanding of the Christian spiritual journey that has yet to be developed. And at no point is that understanding more valuable than in his discussion of the important place our emotions play in helping us discern whether we are choosing God or choosing self.

St. Ignatius suggests that the core task involved in developing a discerning heart is learning to attend to the ways in which we are affected by either turning toward or away from God. We are, as we have already noted, always in God's presence. Because God cloaks his grandeur for our protection, our response to God's presence is not usually the Damascus Road knocked-off-our-feet-and-struck-blind experience of Paul (Acts 9:1-9). Typically, God's presence is more subtle, and our reactions are correspondingly attenuated.

You may, for example, notice that when your heart is turned to God and you are aware of divine love, you are filled with a sense of deep peace and well-being. An awareness of God's presence and love may give you a sense of love for others—possibly a heightened sense of compassion or keener awareness of the fundamental connectedness that exists between you and all other persons. Or it may simply be that awareness of God gives you a sense of vitality, an impulse to live life more fully and with more passion.

Consolation is the name St. Ignatius gave to these feelings that come as gifts of God's gracious presence. It is the way our souls light up when we turn toward God and find ourselves aligned in our depths with Ultimate Reality. It is the coming alive that we experience when we are in the presence of Grace and Truth. It assures us that all is well because we are held in the arms of Everlasting Love. It calls us outside and beyond ourselves to serve others in love and with creativity and passion. It calls us to God.

But once you begin to become aware of these feelings that come from having your face turned toward God, you will also begin to

be aware of a corresponding but entirely opposite set of feelings—
desolation. These are the feelings that you will notice if you prayerfully attend to what happens in your depths when you turn away
from God. You may, for example, notice yourself becoming more
self-preoccupied, more negative, drained of energy, or even mildly
depressed or irritable. What is happening to you is that as you turn
away from God, your borders become smaller and your soul shrivels
and shudders. What you are experiencing is the early indication
that you are on a downward spiral of death.

My most telltale sign of desolation is usually a low-level sense
of anxiety. As I have come to understand the spiritual significance
of these feelings of unease, I have learned to view them as a signal
that I have turned my face from God to myself. My apprehension
about an important upcoming meeting lets me see that having
done what I could to prepare, I am choosing to take responsibility
for the outcome of something over which I have no control.
Turning toward God, I then gently place that meeting in his hands
and surrender my much-loved posture of control and responsibility.

Similarly, the distress I feel when someone I respect is critical of
something I have written is a signal that I love my glittering image
of myself more than I love God. It calls me to turn to God and
re-align my heart with God's heart.

Sometimes feelings of desolation are an indication that there is
something in the experience, person or choice I am facing that
does not hold life for me. Desolation is at these times a divine
nudge toward awareness that there is something not right for me
in what I am considering, at least not right for me at the present
moment. At other times, feelings of desolation are an indication
that something I love more than God has displaced God from the
center of my heart. Desolation is, in this situation, a sign of a disordered desire (sometimes called a disordered attachment). Let me
give an example of each of these.

DESOLATION AS A NUDGE TOWARD A BETTER CHOICE

I mentioned in the preface that I resisted writing this book. While I had thought about it as a possibility, I was tired of facing my own willfulness and wanted to write on something else. I started a book on solitude and stillness. But that was the book I wanted to write, not the one God wanted. That became clear to me through an experience of desolation.

When I am in tune with God's Spirit, my writing and other activities leave me feeling energized, whole, connected and alive. I have a sense of being open to God and carried along by the river of God's loving will and presence. I feel at one with God, myself and life.

This was not my experience as I began writing the book on solitude and stillness. How ironic, I thought, that I was writing about inner stillness and yet experiencing nothing of what I was describing. I had known deep stillness before—increasingly, in fact, in recent years. Why not now?

My willfulness didn't allow me to wait for the obvious answer. I kept plowing ahead, excited about what I was writing and allowing this to distract me from the growing sense of inner disquiet.

Finally I could do so no longer. The turbulence in my soul demanded prayerful attention. I set aside a day for discernment, asking God to help me understand what was going on. The answer was as clear as if God had sent me an email or picked up the phone and made a call: "That book may be a good idea, but it's not my idea—at least not for now."

Immediately I felt relief. Immediately I closed the Word document I had been working on and moved it to the folder called "Book Ideas." That book may be completed someday, but it was clearly not what I should be writing at the present moment.

What a gift this nudge of desolation was to me. It was an invitation to notice my willful self-determination—to write about what I wanted to write about. It was an invitation to choose the better way—to reconnect with Life and to surrender to God's loving will for me.

I do not mean to imply that we need to discern God's will about every little decision that we face—which clothes to put on in the morning or what to cook for dinner. That trivializes God's will. But God's care for us extends to even the small details of life, and sometimes desolation will be given as a gift to call us to a better choice—something more in harmony with God's loving and perfect will for us at that moment.

DESOLATION AS A SIGN OF DISORDERED DESIRE

A more important matter of discernment in my life can illustrate the second form of desolation, a warning about disordered desire.

For the last year my wife and I have been considering a major move—leaving Canada and moving abroad. Several possibilities are under consideration, none of which were sought out but each of which seems to hold attractive possibilities. Weighing the costs—including leaving family and friends and a network of deeply fulfilling work responsibilities—against the opportunities— a chance to reduce our travel while sharpening the focus of our work—has not been easy. So we have left ourselves lots of time to discern God's will and decide what to do.

Our discernment process has included a number of elements— rational examination of the pros and cons of each option, extensive prayer and conversation about the possibilities, seeking the advice of spiritual friends and directors. We have also agreed to remain attentive to God's movement in our souls as we consider either moving or staying, and one possible move versus another.

It has been attentiveness to the rhythms of consolation and desolation that has, for each of us, been most instructive to this point. Focusing on one option at a time, we have allowed ourselves several weeks to assume that we would move, followed by several more weeks to assume that we would not. These weeks were not to be filled with further rational analysis of the decision. This had already been done and had not been particularly helpful. This was time to simply live as if we were moving, or not moving, to one particular place and see what happened in our spirit.

The result has been quite dramatic—at least in the case of one possible move. Both of us felt agitated, anxious and troubled during the weeks when we assumed that we would accept this particular opportunity and make this particular move. The next weeks produced the exact opposite; we both felt relief, peace and a strong sense of being settled in God.

What was the desolation I experienced around this possible option telling me? My discovery (and this being my story, I will tell only what God's nudge of desolation meant for me) was that if I had chosen this opportunity I would have been doing so for wrong and spiritually dangerous reasons.

My desolation revealed disordered desires. What I discovered in prayerful reflection was that my attraction to this particular option was based principally on my inordinate desire for adventure and change and, to a lesser extent, my desire for comfort and security. These desires are not bad in themselves, but they were bad for me at this time because I was putting them in a place of ultimacy—desiring them more than God and God's will for me. Choosing on the basis of these disordered desires would have been spiritually disastrous.

It might have been possible to choose this particular option for other reasons. But my pattern of desolation corresponded to that of my wife, and we both felt relief when we turned the option down. Our discernment process continues around the other possibilities. We both remain open to God's leading. But more important, we both seek to remain open to God and to the alignment of our hearts with the divine heart. This is what I most truly and deeply desire. My desire for adventure, change, comfort and security are derivatives of this core desire—derivatives that enrich life when they are subservient to my fundamental life orientation but that are spiritually dangerous when they become disordered.

Discernment is learning to be attentive to these subtle movements and countermovements toward and away from God. Attending to the feelings that predictably correspond to each heart direction can help us discern God's will. By learning to recognize the markers of having turned away from God, we can learn to more quickly and fully turn toward God. The self-focus that is a part of discernment is the means to the end, but not the end. The point of developing a discerning heart is to focus on God. It is a tool to help us learn to choose God.

Going with the Flow

Ultimately we can discern consolation and desolation only in relation to our basic heart allegiances. A metaphor suggested by Margaret Silf is helpful here.

Consolation and desolation both have to do with our basic life orientation—either away from or toward God. Think of movement away from God as swimming upstream in a river against the current, and movement toward God as floating downstream with the current. Silf explores the dynamics of these two movements:

> For those drifting away from God, the action of God in their lives disturbs them and churns up their moods, creating peacelessness, while the things that come from their own kingdoms make them feel good and leave them apparently contented. For those whose lives are moving toward God, the opposite effects are apparent: when God is touching them,

they feel at peace and they know that somehow they are on solid ground; when they are (hopefully temporarily) attending to their own kingdoms, they feel that they are not really living true and they experience inner turmoil.[4]

Desolation is spiritual turbulence. Although we are highly adept at ignoring it, if we learn to become spiritually attentive and discerning, we notice that we feel churned up from time to time. These are the times when we have taken our eyes off God and turned our backs toward God. In contrast, when we turn toward God in a posture of surrender, we feel instantaneous spiritual peace and consolation. This sense of well-being is much deeper than happiness. One can be happy but in a state of desolation when superficial pleasant feelings block out the dis-ease of a soul in turbulence. But equally important, one can be unhappy yet in a state of profound consolation that offers deep assurance of God's presence in the midst of distress.

Going with the flow of God's kingdom is floating in the river of divine love. This is why the core task involved in developing discernment is learning to pay attention to God's personal love for us. A discerning heart is a heart attentive to God. A discerning spirit is attentive to the differing movements in our depths between those moments when our face is toward God and those when our face is turned away.

In the movie *Chariots of Fire,* Olympic runner Eric Liddell described the relationship between his passion—running—and God's passion: "God made me fast, and when I run I feel his pleasure." This was a man who had a discerning heart. He knew God's pleasure because his own heart was closely aligned with God's. And he was quite right when he said he knew that his running gave God pleasure. The God whose heart he shared was the God who gave him his desire to run.

PRACTICING DISCERNMENT

For Eric Liddell, choosing to run was choosing God and choosing life. For you it may well be something different. The challenge is learning to live close to the heart of God and attentive to your own spirit. Only then will you be able to discern the movements of your own spirit that either mirror or show opposition to the movements of God's Spirit.

Attentiveness to God is aided by attentiveness to the movements of our own spirit. Like many others, I have found the most helpful beginning point for the development of such discernment to be the awareness examen (short for examination of consciousness). Don't be confused by the name. This prayer is actually quite simple. At its core it is a prayerful review of the day—allowing God to bring the important events of the day to mind, much like looking out the window of a moving train and noticing what you see—with an eye toward discerning when we were aware of God's presence and when we were not.[5]

The examen is powerfully aided by attentiveness to periods of consolation (when we felt aligned with God and on solid ground) and periods of desolation (when we felt turbulence) in the day. Prayerfully looking back, we then seek to recall in each type of situation what we were doing, what we were thinking or feeling, and where our heart and attention were in relation to God. Tracking moments of consolation and desolation helps us discern both the deepest desires of our heart and the sources of our deepest dis-ease. Consolation points us toward God's action in our life. Desolation points us toward the action of the kingdom of self.

St. Ignatius, the developer of this prayer review, urged his disciples to practice it every day, even if they did not have time for any other form of prayer. Its importance is that it helps us cultivate a discerning heart. By means of it we learn to align ourselves with

God, moment by moment. This is the core of Christian spirituality. It is the core of willing God's way.

If you have never before practiced the awareness examen, do so for the next week. Allow ten to fifteen minutes each night before going to bed for prayerful reflection on where God was in your day, as evidenced by the movements of your spirit. You will begin to notice the periods of consolation and desolation that are part of every day. Ask God to help you become aware of these as they are occurring during the day. This will give you a chance to choose between life and death, between the kingdom of God and the kingdom of self, moment by moment.

Remember that you are always in God's presence. You do not need to do anything to enter it. Pray for spiritual eyes that will gift you with this awareness throughout your day. This is developing discernment. It is learning to prefer God's will to yours.

Epilogue

The Heart of
the Spiritual Journey

*T*his book has focused on several closely interrelated dimensions of the self, each of which plays an important part in the spiritual journey. We have talked about the will and ways of choosing, about desires and their purification, about love and its transformational potential, and about the alignment of our heart with the heart of God. It is now time to pull these strands together and see how they fit within the overall spiritual journey.

Let's start with the heart because although I have referred to it repeatedly throughout the book, I have yet to define it. Understanding the heart is critical if we are to understand the transformation that is worked in us through Christ-following because the heart lies right at—if I may put it this way—the heart of the Christian spiritual journey.

HEART AND MIND

When I ask Christians what first comes to their mind when I speak the word "heart" many say "evil." They may be remembering the words of the prophet Jeremiah when he spoke of the heart as being desperately wicked and deceitful (Jeremiah 17:9), or Jesus' teaching that it is from the heart that all that is evil emerges (Mark 7:21). It's no wonder they mistrust anything called the heart.

Western culture also provides a set of associations to the non-physical heart that seriously distort its essential nature. Under the influence of Valentine's Day and Hallmark cards, perhaps you think of emotions when I speak of the heart. But the spiritual heart I am referring to has very little to do with personal affectivity and absolutely nothing to do with gushing sentimentality or soft-headedness. It is, therefore, quite different from the heart as understood by both biblical literalists and popular culture.

I draw my understanding of the heart from the perennial wisdom tradition—the tradition that Cynthia Bourgeault and others have argued shaped Jesus' understanding of the inner life and its transformation.[1] Within the wisdom tradition, the heart is the fullness of the mind. It is not, therefore, something that can be reduced to emotions, and rather than being the source of human evil, it is understood as a way of accessing wisdom.

The mind is much more than reason and thought. It also includes such subtle and generally underdeveloped faculties as intuition, imagination, symbol formation, listening to our bodies and attending to our deep emotions, moods and shifting ego states. All these are not *less* than rational but *more than* rational. They are, therefore, transrational. They include reason but transcend and integrate it within other deeper faculties of the heart.

The heart has a bigger perspective than the mind. It can see further than the mind because it draws its data from all levels of reality—including but never limited to the mind. The heart is our spiritual center because it is the seat of imagination and intuition. It is the heart that dreams and through our deepest desires leads us forward. Unlike ego, the heart doesn't perceive by differentiation but by means of its inherent resonance with wholeness, alignment, oneness, harmony, proportion and beauty. There should be no surprise therefore that it is the heart that has long been recognized in spiritual teaching as the core of our being.

We see this understanding and emphasis in the teaching of Jesus that the heart determines everything we do, say and think (Matthew 6:21; Luke 2:19), and that it is the pure in heart that would see God (Matthew 5:8). This is why cleansing of the lens of the heart allows us to see and love God. Summarizing this understanding of the heart, St. Augustine tells us that the whole purpose of life is to restore to health the eye of the heart, for it is by this that God may be seen and known to be within.[2]

The core of the transformational journey is aligning our heart and mind. In Eastern Orthodox Christianity this is described as the journey of the mind down into the heart, something understood to lie at the core of the purification of the passions. Like a bird going back to its nest at the close of the day, the spiritual journey involves the mind settling into its home in the heart, thus allowing it to access the deeper sources of wisdom that it contains. This is what is involved in taking on the heart and mind of Christ. This is the heart of what is involved in allowing our hearts and minds to be aligned with the heart and mind of Christ.[3]

WILL AND DESIRE

The cultivation of the heart—something I often describe as the development of heartfulness—is the route to the transformation of will and desire. The process of discernment that I described in chapter seven is central to the transformation of our choosing and decision making. It is the movement from the egoic way of choosing based on reason that is shaped by desire to choosing that is based on the wisdom of a discerning heart.

God's agenda for change is much more radical than ours. Easily we settle for simply choosing the right thing. God's agenda is much grander. God also wants us to choose the right thing for the right reasons and to make this choice in the right way. This comes about by giving us a heart transplant—the heart of God in exchange for our heart of stony egocentric willfulness. And then God invites us to allow this new heart to lead our choosing, a redeemed heart guiding redeemed choosing.

Although they are easily misunderstood and certainly can be disordered, our deepest desires point us beyond ourselves. But if our longings are again to become God's longings, they must be reset to their default position, with God as the object of our deepest yearning. Only then will we know the freedom of being able to really trust our heart. Only when we desire nothing but God can we truly enjoy all God's other blessings.

The spiritual life is always a unified life, oriented around one basic longing. Christian spirituality is a heart and will unified in Christ and oriented toward the loving Father. Despite our efforts, no one can live in both the kingdom of self and the kingdom of God. To truly live the life of the unseen God is to renounce the desire of all that can be seen. "To possess Him who cannot be understood is to renounce all that can be understood. To rest in Him who is beyond all created rest, we renounce the desire to rest in created things."[4]

Choosing God is, as we have seen, choosing life. Choosing God's will is allowing ourselves to emerge from the cave of our egocentric gratification and come home to the loving Father who patiently waits to throw us a party. How blind we are when we fail to see that God's will is God's dream for us and the world. It is a dream full of abundance. It is a dream of healing and wholeness. It is a dream of life together in the reign of Perfect Love.

PURITY OF HEART

Jesus taught that no one can serve two masters. We can each only have one basic heart allegiance. But so often we live with divided hearts. Purity of heart, Søren Kierkegaard reminds us, is to will one thing. As the mind and heart of Christ become our heart and mind, willfulness becomes willingness. And because heart and mind are now aligned, surrender becomes an act of the heart, not merely the fruit of the will. This is why the heart lies right at the core of Christian spiritual transformation. And this is why the purification of the heart is so central to Christian spiritual formation.

But don't confuse purity of heart with sin avoidance. Purity is alignment and singleness of heart and mind that results from receiving the mind and heart of Christ as our own. But this is where this trilogy of books loops back upon itself—because the mind and heart of Christ are not alien to us but have always been our deepest truth and reality. We could, therefore, describe this taking on of the heart and mind of Christ as actualizing our true self. And how do we do that? By surrendering to the Perfect Love that is our source and destiny.

Having arrived at this point in the book, you likely already know something about this. Perhaps you, like me, have occasionally tasted the joy of surrender to God but then settled back into life in the kingdom of self. Most of the time we don't even notice that we have done this. We are so insensitive to our own spirit that we no longer notice when we have turned away from God's Spirit.

May God help us learn to attend to the movements of our own spirit so that we can attend to the movements of God's Spirit in us. This is the core of choosing God moment by moment. It is the key to true life.

Appendix

For Reflection and Discussion

No one gets very far on the path of Christian spirituality without two things—space for contemplative reflection and engagement with others who share the journey. I have already invited some of the former by offering suggestions for reflection at the end of each chapter. This was a way of encouraging you to take the necessary time to ponder what you were reading.

Now that you have finished the book, let me invite you to once again take time to reflect on what you have read as I offer questions and suggestions suitable for both individuals and groups. I have organized these around two types of groups. The first is a group that meets for four sessions of forty-five minutes, each session discussing two or more chapters. This is followed by a suggested framework for a group that meets only once for seventy-five to ninety minutes for a discussion of the book as a whole. If you are using this Appendix for your own reflection and do not anticipate being part of a group discussion, you can draw from either of these sets of questions.

A Four-Session Discussion Guide to *Desiring God's Will*

~ Session One ~

PREFACE: WILLING GOD'S WAY *AND* CHAPTER 1: WAYS OF WILLING

1. In preparation for this first session let me suggest that you go back through the preface and chapter 1 and make a note of your favorite quotes. Perhaps you have already done this by marking your book, but even so I would still encourage you to mark the two to three selections that most affected you. As you introduce yourself to the others in your group at the start of this first session, share the one quote that most deeply affected you and tell them how you responded to it.

2. How do you honestly feel about God's will? What do you think of when you hear someone talk about its importance? In the preface I suggest that most of us seem to approach it more like cutting back on eating enjoyable foods than following our heart to the Source of abundant life. Which is more true for you? What things have shaped how you approach discerning and surrendering to God's will?

3. Talk about compliance with God's will tends to trigger our will—sometimes in willing surrender but more often in either willful resistance or willful attempts at compliance. Think about other ways of choosing that have led to important decisions and actions in your life where your choice was made more by your heart than your will. Share an example of this with the group; after others have done the same, discuss the differences between choosing with the will and choosing with the heart. What are the limitations and advantages of each?

4. What do you know of the dark side of willfulness? Find examples of ways of deciding and living willfully from different stages of your life and notice if your reliance on your will has changed since childhood. Do you agree that "as a naked force of self-propulsion, willfulness is both spiritually and psychologically destructive"? Why has it so often been foundational to how we think about Christ-following?

5. Notice the difference in your life—spiritually and psychologically—when you act *against* something in contrast to acting *for* something. How does this relate to choosing by means of the will or heart?

6. On a ten-point scale, how would you rate your investment in control in the last year? How would this compare to ten years ago? Do you agree that rigidity and investment in control are signs of opposition to life? How does your spirituality make you either more or less open to life?

7. How do you understand the way in which willfulness and pride go together? Think of some examples from your life and the lives of others that help you understand this relationship.

8. What positive role can discipline play in the spiritual life? What role does discipline play in yours?

~ Session Two ~

CHAPTER 2: MY KINGDOM, THY KINGDOM *AND* CHAPTER 3: LOVE AND WILL

1. In preparation for this session let me again suggest that you go back through chapters 2 and 3 and identify your favorite quotes. To start this second session, share your most important takeaway from session 1 and the one quote that most deeply affected you from these two chapters—and how you have responded to it.

2. Slowly and reflectively, reread the Lord's Prayer found near the beginning of chapter 2. How does it, and the discussion in that chapter, help you understand the difference between your kingdom and God's kingdom? What do you notice in this prayer that you may have never previously noticed? How might it change how you pray this prayer in the future?

3. How do you respond to the kingdom exercise of St. Ignatius found in the "Thy Kingdom Come" section of chapter 2? Make time to meditate on it for ten minutes for each of the next three days and notice how your response develops. Share your experience with the group and discuss the challenge of helping people hear the invitation, not the command, in Christ's call to follow him.

4. Reflectively review the discussion found in the "The Freedom of Surrender" section of chapter 2 about Jesus' mother Mary and the way her consent to God's will leads to freedom. What can you learn from Mary?

5. Borrowing from Rollo May, I suggest at the beginning of chapter 3 that "without love, willpower is often little more than

a twisted, self-centered demonstration of one's own character." The twisting of character that I refer to is the false self, which is reinforced by acts of willpower that are devoid of love. Think of examples of how you have exercised such loveless willpower to see if you can identify how this strengthened your false self and share these with the group.

6. In what domains of your life do you continue to choose to stay comfortably within the kingdom of self and resist surrender to the kingdom of God? Be as honest as you can in answering this. Don't be distracted by guilt. Simply acknowledge where you are and speak this truth to God. Share as much of this truth as you are willing to share with the group.

7. Chapter 3 discusses what I describe as "Love-Shaped Willing" and "Willingness as Consent." What examples of this can you find in your interactions with others or your own life? What can you learn from Joseph about surrender as willing consent?

8. Close this second session by praying together the Lord's Prayer. Speak the words with openness and faith as an expression of your intent and as an offering of your consent, even if at this moment they do not yet fully reflect your willingness to choose God's loving will.

~ *Session Three* ~

CHAPTER 4: CHOOSING GOD *AND* CHAPTER 5: WILL AND DESIRE

1. In preparation for this session let me again suggest that you go back through chapters 4 and 5 and identify your favorite quotes. To start this third session, share your most important take-

away from session 2 and the one quote that most deeply affected you from chapters 4 and 5—and how you have responded to it.

2. To what extent have you tended to think of God's will in terms of choices at major decision points in life rather than God's dream for you? How would you respond differently to God's will if you truly believed that it was God's dream for you—an expression of God's boundless love of you and hope for the fullness of your being that comes from knowing and living out of that love?

3. Listen again to the words of Psalm 5:3: "I say this prayer to you, Yahweh, for at daybreak you listen for my voice; and at dawn I hold myself in readiness for you, I watch for you." How would your attentiveness to God's presence be different if you began each morning with this prayer? Try it for a few days and share your experience with the group. Think of these days as days of practicing the presence of God. How does this practice affect your openness to God?

4. Reread Simone Weil's understanding of the importance of awareness as a transformational power found in the section "Will and Awareness" in chapter 4. How could awareness be more powerful than will as a force of change? Have you ever experienced this? Weil also argues that transformation happens when we allow ourselves to desire something, not simply when we try to accomplish or obtain it. What role might desires have in our Christ-following? How might they increase your receptive openness and influence your intentions?

5. What has been your experience of God's seeming absence? What have you begun to learn about God's presence in these experiences of darkness? How might knowing and trusting God's presence influence your choosing of God's will?

6. What do you know about being led by your heart, not simply your will? What problems could be associated with choosing with the heart? How can will be shaped by love and in so doing, be brought down into the heart?

7. Discuss the quote from Thomas Merton offered in the section "The Heart's Desires" in chapter 5: "Life is shaped by the end you live for. You are made in the image of what you desire." What desires have shaped your life? Why do we tend to doubt that desires are spiritual and as important potential reflections of God's movement within our depths?

8. Chapter 5 discusses the role of prayer in the purification of desires. What keeps you from bringing your desires into this place of Divine purification and reordering? What do you know of the way in which this can be the place in which God's heart becomes your heart?

~ *Session Four* ~

CHAPTER 6: CHOOSING THE CROSS, CHAPTER 7: DEVELOPING A DISCERNING HEART *AND* EPILOGUE: THE HEART OF THE SPIRITUAL JOURNEY

1. In preparation for this final session let me again suggest that you go back through chapters 6, 7 and the epilogue to identify your favorite quotes. To start this final session, share your most important take-away from session 3 and the one quote that most deeply affected you from chapters 6, 7 and the epilogue— and how you have responded to it.

2. Based on your experience do you agree that the church has

often minimized the costs of Christ-following? What have been the consequences of watered-down versions of Christian spirituality that fail to place the cross at the center of the journey? Understood as the instruments of our crucifixion, not merely the cause of minor annoyance, what inner crosses have been heaviest for you to carry on your journey?

3. What have you learned about embracing your crosses as a means of meeting God in transformational ways? Share this with the group and listen carefully to the experience of others when you discuss this question in this final session.

4. What have you been taught about the place of emotions in Christianity? Do you agree that emotions have a very important role in spirituality? If not, why not? If you do agree, what has been lost as a result of the church's general neglect of the important role of emotions in human well-being? What overall message about the role of emotions in spirituality have you most strongly heard or been taught?

5. In the section "Emotions and Spirituality" in chapter 7, three levels of emotion are identified: superficial feelings, moods and deeper emotions, and the generally quite rare experiences of peak experiences and unitive knowing. Review the discussion of these three levels of affect and notice the extent of your experience at each level. What do you know of your deeper feelings that lie in what I describe as the intermediate zone? How have you learned to identify and listen to these deeper feelings? What, if anything, have you known of the peak experiences discussed in this section? How important do you think knowing your deeper emotions is in the purification of our desires? What other things do you think are helpful in this process?

6. St. Ignatius suggests that the core task involved in developing a discerning heart is learning to attend to the ways in which you

are affected by either turning toward or away from God; review this idea in the "Consolation and Desolation" section in chapter 7. How do you experience desolation, as understood by St. Ignatius? How do you experience consolation? How might this help you discern the movements of God's spirit in your heart?

7. The epilogue places the major ideas and practices presented in this book back into the larger context of the Christian spiritual journey, arguing that the heart of that journey is the transformation of our heart. How do you respond to the understanding of the heart and mind presented in the epilogue? What holds you back from a life of heartfulness in which your mind rests in your heart, which is now the very heart of God?

8. Reflect on the gifts and invitations that you feel have come from the Spirit of God to you through the study and discussion of this book. How will you respond to them? What is your next step in offering your full-hearted consent to what God is offering as you continue to walk this path of Christ-following?

A One-Session Discussion Guide to *Desiring God's Will*

1. How do you honestly feel about God's will? What do you think of when you hear someone talk about its importance? In the preface I suggest that most of us seem to approach it more like cutting back on eating enjoyable foods than following our heart to the Source of abundant life. Which is more true for you? What things have shaped how you approach discerning and surrendering to God's will?

2. What do you know of the dark side of willfulness? Find examples of ways of deciding and living willfully from different stages of your life and notice if your reliance on your will has changed since childhood. Do you agree that "as a naked force of self-propulsion, willfulness is both spiritually and psychologically destructive"? Why has it so often been foundational to how we think about Christ-following?

3. Notice the difference in your life—spiritually and psychologically—when you act *against* something in contrast to acting *for* something. How does this relate to choosing by means of the will or heart?

4. What positive role can discipline play in the spiritual life? What role does discipline play in yours?

5. How do you respond to the kingdom exercise of St. Ignatius

found in the "Thy Kingdom Come" section of chapter 2? Make time to meditate on it for ten minutes for each of the next three days and notice how your response develops. Share your experience with the group and discuss the challenge of helping people hear the invitation, not the command, in Christ's call to follow him.

6. Chapter 3 discusses what I describe as "Love-Shaped Willing" and "Willingness as Consent." What examples of this can you find in your interactions with others or your own life? What can you learn from Joseph about surrender as willing consent?

7. To what extent have you tended to think of God's will in terms of choices at major decision points in life rather than God's dream for you? How would you respond differently to God's will if you truly believed that it was God's dream for you—an expression of God's boundless love of you and hope for the fullness of your being that comes from knowing and living out of that love?

8. Reread Simone Weil's understanding of the importance of awareness as a transformational power found in the section "Will and Awareness" in chapter 4. How could awareness be more powerful than will as a force of change? Have you ever experienced this? Weil also argues that transformation happens when we allow ourselves to desire something, not simply when we try to accomplish or obtain it. What role might desires have in our Christ-following? How might they increase your receptive openness and influence your intentions?

9. What has been your experience of God's seeming absence? What have you begun to learn about God's presence in these experiences of darkness? How might knowing and trusting God's presence influence your choosing of God's will?

10. What do you know about being led by your heart, not simply your will? What problems could be associated with choosing with the heart? How can will be shaped by love and in so doing, be brought down into the heart?

11. Chapter 5 discusses the role of prayer in the purification of desires. What keeps you from bringing your desires into this place of Divine purification and reordering? What do you know of the way in which this can be the place in which God's heart becomes your heart?

12. What have you learned about embracing your crosses as a means of meeting God in transformational ways? Share this with the group and listen carefully to the experience of others when you discuss this question in this final session.

13. St. Ignatius suggests that the core task involved in developing a discerning heart is learning to attend to the ways in which you are affected by either turning toward or away from God; review this idea in the "Consolation and Desolation" section in chapter 7. How do you experience desolation, as understood by St. Ignatius? How do you experience consolation? How might this help you discern the movements of God's spirit in your heart?

14. In the section "Emotions and Spirituality" in chapter 7, three levels of emotion are identified: superficial feelings, moods and deeper emotions, and the generally quite rare experiences of peak experiences and unitive knowing. Review the discussion of these three levels of affect and notice the extent of your experience at each level. What do you know of your deeper feelings that lie in what I describe as the intermediate zone? How have you learned to identify and listen to these deeper feelings? What, if anything, have you known of the peak experiences discussed in this section? How important do you think knowing

your deeper emotions is in the purification of our desires? What other things do you think are helpful in this process?

15. Reflect on the gifts and invitations that you feel have come from the Spirit of God to you through the study and discussion of this book. How will you respond to them? What is your next step in cooperating with the Spirit of God as you continue the transformational journey of Christ-following?

16. Close the session by praying together the Lord's Prayer. Speak the words with openness and faith as an expression of your intent and as an offering of your consent, even if at this moment they do not yet fully reflect your willingness to choose God's loving will.

Notes

Preface: Willing God's Way

[1]David G. Benner, *Surrender to Love: Discovering the Heart of Christian Spirituality* (Downers Grove, IL: InterVarsity Press, 2015), and *The Gift of Being Yourself: The Sacred Call to Self-Discovery* (Downers Grove, IL: InterVarsity Press, 2015).

Chapter 1: Ways of Willing

[1]Herman Melville, *Moby Dick*, Great Books of the Western World 48 (Chicago: Encyclopaedia Britannica, 1952), 123.
[2]Ibid.
[3]Erik Erikson, *Childhood and Society* (New York: W. W. Norton, 1963), 252.
[4]Kenneth Boa, *Conformed to His Image* (Grand Rapids: Zondervan, 2001), 79.
[5]Ibid.

Chapter 2: My Kingdom, Thy Kingdom

[1]Louis Evely, *We Make Bold to Say Our Father*, trans. James Langdale (New York: Herder & Herder, 1965), 11.
[2]Ibid., 25.
[3]Ibid., 11.
[4]Simone Weil, *Simone Weil: An Anthology*, ed. and trans. Siân Miles (New York: Grove, 1986), 216.
[5]I base my adaptation of this exercise on David Fleming, *Draw Me into Your Friendship: A Literal Translation and Contemporary Reading of the Spiritual Exercises* (St. Louis: Institute of Jesuit Sources, 1996).
[6]Origen, *De Oratione*, quoted in *Catechism of the Catholic Church* (Ottawa: Canadian Conference of Catholic Bishops, 1992), 572.
[7]Evely, *We Make Bold*, 71.

[8]Ibid., 76.

[9]Dallas Willard, *The Divine Conspiracy* (San Francisco: HarperSanFrancisco, 1998), 21.

[10]Ibid., 15.

CHAPTER 3: LOVE AND WILL

[1]Rollo May, *Love and Will* (New York: W. W. Norton, 1969), 216-22.

[2]Ibid., 276.

[3]Leslie Farber, *The Ways of the Will: Selected Essays* (New York: BasicBooks, 2000), 79.

[4]Although the Gospels affirm that Joseph had no part in Mary's conception of Jesus, they present Joseph as Jesus' father without any further qualification (Luke 2:33, 48; John 1:45; 6:42).

CHAPTER 4: CHOOSING GOD

[1]Brother Lawrence, *The Practice of the Presence of God* (New York: Harper & Row, 1941).

[2]Frank Laubach, *Practicing His Presence* (Goleta, CA: Christian Books, 1976), 5.

[3]Richard Norris, *Understanding the Faith of the Church* (New York: Seabury, 1979), 10-11.

[4]Richard Rohr, *Everything Belongs: The Gift of Contemplative Prayer* (New York: Crossroad, 1999), 28.

[5]Simone Weil, *Simone Weil: An Anthology*, ed. and trans. Siân Miles (New York: Grove, 1986), 212.

[6]Ibid., 213.

[7]Ibid., 213-14.

[8]Like most Hasidic stories, this one comes from oral tradition. My account is based on a version presented by *The Virtual Rebbe*, www.hasidicstories .com/Articles/Learning_From_Stories/virtual.html.

[9]Gordon Smith, *Listening to God in Times of Choice: The Art of Discerning God's Will* (Downers Grove, IL: InterVarsity Press, 1997), 149.

[10]Gray Temple, *When God Happens* (New York: Church Publishing, 2001), 5.

[11]Louis Evely, *This Man Is You* (New York: Paulist, 1964), 26-27.

[12]Ibid., 15.

[13]Anonymous, *The Cloud of Unknowing*, ed. James Walsh (New York: Paulist, 1981), 139.

[14]Evely, *This Man Is You,* 8.

CHAPTER 5: WILL AND DESIRE

[1]Margaret Silf, *Inner Compass: An Invitation to Ignatian Spirituality* (Chicago: Loyola Press, 1999), 75.

[2]Thomas Merton, *Thoughts in Solitude* (Boston: Shambhala, 1993), 55.

[3]Fiona Bowie, ed., *Beguine Spirituality,* trans. Oliver Davies (New York: Crossroad, 1990), 55-56.

[4]Janet Ruffing, *Spiritual Direction: Beyond the Beginnings* (New York: Paulist, 2000), 11.

[5]Merton, *Thoughts in Solitude,* 89.

CHAPTER 6: CHOOSING THE CROSS

[1]Francis A. Schaeffer. *The God Who Is There* (Downers Grove, IL: InterVarsity Press, 1968).

[2]Richard Rohr, "Religion/Spirituality and Pain: Seeking an Icon of Transformation," *Journal of Christian Healing* 22, no. 1-2 (Spring/Summer 2000): 52.

[3]Ibid., 53.

[4]Joseph Campbell, *The Power of Myth,* PBS Television, broadcast 1988.

CHAPTER 7: DEVELOPING A DISCERNING HEART

[1]I base this approach to levels of emotion and their role in discernment on a model of discernment presented in Pierre Wolff, *Discernment: The Art of Choosing Well* (Ligouri, MO: Triumph, 1993).

[2]Gerald May, *Will and Spirit: A Contemplative Psychology* (San Francisco: Harper & Row, 1983), 53.

[3]Henri J. M. Nouwen, *The Way of the Heart: Desert Spirituality and Contemporary Ministry* (San Francisco: Harper & Row, 1981).

[4]Margaret Silf, *Inner Compass: An Invitation to Ignatian Spirituality* (Chicago: Loyola Press, 1999), 41.

[5]See David G. Benner, *Sacred Companions: The Gift of Spiritual Friendship and Direction* (Downers Grove, IL: InterVarsity Press, 2002), 113-15, for a fuller discussion of this spiritual discipline.

EPILOGUE: THE HEART OF THE SPIRITUAL JOURNEY

[1]Cynthia Bourgeault, *The Wisdom Jesus: Transforming Heart and Mind—A*

New Perspective on Christ and His Message (Boston: Shambhala, 2008). For further discussion of the heart from the perspective of the wisdom tradition, see also Cynthia Bourgeault, *The Wisdom Way of Knowing: Reclaiming an Ancient Tradition to Awaken the Heart* (San Francisco: Jossey-Bass, 2003).

[2]Quoted in Whitall N. Perry, *A Treasury of Traditional Wisdom* (San Francisco: Harper & Row, 1986), 819.

[3]See David G. Benner, *Human Being and Becoming* (Grand Rapids: Brazos Press, forthcoming) for more extensive discussion of the heart and mind, and of the transformational journey of bringing the mind down into the heart and living with the abundant heartfulness that comes from this.

[4]Thomas Merton, *Thoughts in Solitude* (Boston: Shambhala, 1993), 55.

About the Author

*D*r. David G. Benner is an internationally known depth psychologist and transformational coach whose life's work has been directed toward helping people walk the human path in a deeply spiritual way and the spiritual path in a deeply human way. His passion and calling has been the understanding and pursuit of transformation—not merely healing or even growth, but the unfolding of the self associated with a journey of awakening.

David has held faculty appointments at York University, University of Toronto, McMaster University, Redeemer University College, Wheaton College, Psychological Studies Institute at Richmont Graduate University, the Centre for Studies in Religion and Society at University of Victoria and the Living School for Action and Contemplation. He has also served as visiting lecturer at universities in thirty countries and is the author or editor of more than twenty-five books that have been translated into nineteen foreign languages.

Beyond his work in psychology and spirituality David's other principal interests are sailing, cycling, hiking, jazz, good food and soulful conversation. He is married to Juliet Benner, author of

Contemplative Vision: A Guide to Christian Art and Prayer (Inter-Varsity Press). They divide their time between Toronto, Canada, and Lima, Peru.

David can be found online at

- www.drdavidgbenner.ca
- www.facebook.com/drdavidgbenner
- Twitter: @drdavidgbenner

Books by
David G. Benner

Presence and Encounter: The Sacramental Possibilities of Everyday Life (Brazos Press, 2014)

Spirituality and the Awakening Self: The Sacred Journey of Transformation (Brazos Press, 2012)

Soulful Spirituality: Becoming Fully Alive and Deeply Human (Brazos Press, 2011)

Opening to God: Lectio Divina and Life as Prayer (InterVarsity Press, 2010)

Desiring God's Will: Aligning Our Hearts with the Heart of God (InterVarsity Press, 2005)

The Gift of Being Yourself: The Sacred Call to Self-Discovery (InterVarsity Press, 2004)

Spiritual Direction and the Care of Souls: A Guide to Christian Approaches and Practices, ed. with Gary Moon (InterVarsity Press, 2004)

Surrender to Love: *Discovering the Heart of Christian Spirituality* (InterVarsity Press, 2003)

Strategic Pastoral Counseling: A Short-Term Structured Model, 2nd ed. (Baker, 2003)

Sacred Companions: The Gift of Spiritual Friendship and Direction (InterVarsity Press, 2002)

Free at Last: Breaking the Bondage of Guilt and Emotional Wounds (Essence, 1999)

Care of Souls: Reuniting the Psychological and Spiritual for Christian Nurture and Counsel (Baker, 1998)

Money Madness and Financial Freedom: The Psychology of Money Meanings and Management (Detselig, 1996)

Choosing the Gift of Forgiveness, with Robert Harvey (Baker, 1996)

Understanding and Facilitating Forgiveness, with Robert Harvey (Baker, 1996)

Christian Perspectives on Human Development, ed. with Leroy Aden and J. Harold Ellens (Baker, 1992)

Healing Emotional Wounds (Baker, 1990)

Counseling and the Human Predicament, ed. with Leroy Aden (Baker, 1989)

Psychology and Religion, ed. (Baker, 1988)

Psychotherapy and the Spiritual Quest (Baker, 1988)

Psychotherapy in Christian Perspective, ed. (Baker, 1987)

Christian Counseling and Psychotherapy, ed. (Baker, 1987)

Baker Encyclopedia of Psychology, ed. (Baker, 1985)

*f*ormatio

TRADITION. EXPERIENCE.
TRANSFORMATION.

Formatio books from InterVarsity Press follow the rich tradition of the church in the journey of spiritual formation. These books are not merely about being informed, but about being transformed by Christ and conformed to his image. Formatio stands in InterVarsity Press's evangelical publishing tradition by integrating God's Word with spiritual practice and by prompting readers to move from inward change to outward witness. InterVarsity Press uses the chambered nautilus for Formatio, a symbol of spiritual formation because of its continual spiral journey outward as it moves from its center. We believe that each of us is made with a deep desire to be in God's presence. Formatio books help us to fulfill our deepest desires and to become our true selves in light of God's grace.